W9-CGX-425

Illustrated Book of Jesus

Edited by:
Fr. Michael Sullivan
Archdiocese of New York

Christ History & Devotions
Julie Cragon
Nashville, Tenn.

Artwork pages 100 & 154 by Manuel Gervasini

Novenas to The Sacred Heart & Infant of Prague
Fr. Daniel Lord, S.J.
Imprimatur: Francis Cardinal Spellman
Archbishop of New York
1947

Stations of the Cross
Composed by
Saint Alphonse Ligouri
Imprimatur: James Cardinal Gibbons
Archbishop of Baltimore
May 17, 1889

Copyright © 2011 William J. Hirten Co.
Graphics © Fratelli Bonella S.r.l. Milan, Italy

William J. Hirten Co.
35 Industrial Rd.
Cumberland, RI

Illustrated Book
of Jesus

INTRODUCTION

Jesus Christ is the central figure of Christianity. From the information we read in the four Gospels, Jesus was conceived by the Holy Spirit, born of the Virgin Mary and baptized by St. John the Baptist. He was a preacher, a teacher and a healer. He was crucified in Jerusalem under Pontius Pilate, rose from the dead and ascended into Heaven. We believe He was a man like us in all things but sin. His many different titles have developed from His personal life, His places of honor in the life of the Church and His revelations to many holy men and holy women of Faith. Christians honor Jesus as God the Son, one of the three Divine Persons of the Trinity. Devotions to Jesus have developed through the writings of the saints and the Church Fathers and also through the religious experiences, miracles and healings of many of the saints. We honor Jesus with these special devotions and through our meditations on His life and our many traditional prayers that glorify His Holy Name.

The Annunciation

The Angelus

The Angel of the Lord declared unto Mary.

R. And she conceived by the Holy Ghost.

Hail, Mary, etc.

V. Behold the handmaid of the Lord.

R. Be it done unto me accoarding to Thy word.

Hail, Mary, etc.

V. AND THE WORD WAS MADE FLESH.

R. And dwell among us, Hail, Mary, etc.

V. Pray for us, O Holy Mother of God.

R. That we may be made worthy of the promises of Christ.

LET US PRAY

Pour forth, we beseech Thee, O Lord, Thy grace into our hearts; that we to whom the Incarnation of Christ, Thy Son, was made known by the message of an angel, may by His Passion and Cross, be brought to the glory of His Resurrection through the same Christ our Lord.

Amen.

The Annunciation

The Annunciation, as told in the Gospel of Luke, is the announcement by the angel Gabriel to Mary of Nazareth in Galilee, "a virgin betrothed to a man named Joseph, of the house of David," that she will be the mother of Jesus.

Although Mary is "greatly troubled," the angel Gabriel assures her that she should not be afraid and that she has "found favor with God."

When the angel tells her that she will give birth to God's Son, she questions how this can happen since she has never been with a man. As the angel assures her of the "power of the Most High," he also announces that her relative Elizabeth, who was believed to be "barren", has conceived and is in her sixth month.

The announcements from Gabriel to Zechariah about Elizabeth conceiving and to Mary about her conception share moments of uncertainty turning to signs that could come only through the power of God. Mary's "yes" reflects her belief too that certainly "nothing is impossible for God."

She shows her complete trust in God when she says, "I am the handmaid of the Lord." She gives herself completely over to Him for the sake of bringing us a Savior.

The Catechism of the Catholic Church explains that the Annunciation to Mary is the formal beginning of "the time of fulfillment of God's promises and preparations."

The Annunciation is the beginning of Jesus as man. The Feast of the Annunciation is celebrated March 25, exactly nine months before the Birth of Jesus and is the first Joyful Mystery of the Rosary.

The Visitation

The Visitation Prayer

Eternal Father,
You inspired the Virgin Mary,
mother of Your Son,
to visit Elizabeth
and assist her in her need.
Keep us open
to the working of Your Spirit,
and with Mary may
we praise You for ever.
We ask this through
our Lord Jesus Christ,
Your Son who lives
and reigns with You
and the Holy Spirit, one God,
for ever and ever.
Amen.

The Visitation

After the angel Gabriel appears to Mary and announces that she will be the Mother of Jesus and that Elizabeth, her relative, has also conceived a son, Mary travels in haste to visit Elizabeth. We find it very appropriate for the young mother-to-be to go and take care of the expectant mother who is advanced in years.

When Mary arrives and greets Elizabeth, the baby in her womb, John, the one who will make way for Jesus, leaps for joy, aware of the presence of Jesus. The Gospel of Luke tells us that Elizabeth also responds to the presence of Jesus and through the Holy Spirit realizes the greatness of the child carried by Mary, "And how does this happen to me that the Mother of my Lord should come to me?" Mary then expresses her gratefulness in the Magnificat and through this prayer acknowledges all the graces she and the long lines that have gone before her in faith have been given by God. "My soul proclaims the greatness of the Lord; my spirit rejoices in God my savior. For he has looked upon his handmaid's lowliness; behold, from now on will all ages call me blessed.

The Mighty One has done great things for me, and holy is his name." The Visitation is a confirmation that Mary's 'yes' is a blessing and that her entire life, as well as the lives of Elizabeth and John, lead us to Her Son, Jesus. Mary stays with Elizabeth for about three months.

The Feast of the Visitation is celebrated May 31 and is the second Joyful Mystery of the Rosary.

The Nativity

Nativity Prayer

The feast day of your birth resembles You, Lord because it brings joy to all humanity.

Old people and infants alike enjoy your day. Your day is celebrated from generation to generation. Kings and emperors may pass away, and the festivals to commemorate them soon lapse.

But your festival will be remembered until the end of time. Your day is a means and a pledge of peace. At Your birth heaven and earth were reconciled. Since You came from heaven to earth on that day, You forgave our sins and wiped away our guilt.

You gave us so many gifts on the day of Your birth: a treasure chest of spiritual medicines for the sick; Spiritual light for the blind; The cup of salvation for the thirsty; The bread of life for the hungry. In the winter when trees are bare, You give us the most succulent spiritual fruit.

In the frost when the earth is barren, You bring new hope to our souls. In December when seeds are hidden in the soil, the staff of life springs forth from the virgin womb.

Amen.

The Birth of Christ

he story of the Birth of Christ is told in the Gospel of Matthew and the Gospel of Luke.

Both accounts reveal that Jesus is the Son of Mary, betrothed to Joseph. In the Gospel of Luke, Mary is told by the angel Gabriel that she will give birth to a Son and she is to name Him Jesus.

The Child is conceived in her womb by the power of the Holy Spirit. Mary responds, "May it be done to me according to your word."

In the Gospel of Matthew, an angel appears to Joseph in a dream and tells him to take Mary as his wife and to name the Baby, Jesus.

Because they have to register in the census, Joseph takes Mary from Nazareth to Bethlehem which is his ancestral home.

They try to find a place to stay but the inns are already filled. Mary gives birth to Jesus in a stable and places the baby in a manger, an animal feeding trough. An angel then announces the birth of Jesus to shepherds in the field, "For today in the city of David a savior has been born for you who is Messiah and Lord." They travel to see the newborn King and tell everyone what has been told to them.

In Matthew, a star leads a group of magi to Bethlehem to bring gifts to the child Jesus.

The Magi are warned in a dream not to return to Herod and tell about the birth of Jesus. Joseph too is told to take his family and flee to Egypt as soon as Mary and Jesus can travel.

The Birth of Christ is celebrated on Christmas Day and is the third Joyful Mystery of the Rosary.

The Epiphany

Epiphany Prayer

Dear Jesus,
as You led the Three Kings
to You by the light of a star,
please draw us ever closer to You
by the light of Faith.
Help us to desire You
as ardently as they did.
Give us the grace to overcome
all the obstacles
that keep us far from You.
May we, like them,
have something to give You
when we appear before You.
Amen.

The Epiphany

The Epiphany of Jesus is the feast celebrated January 6 commemorating the visit of the Magi to the Baby Jesus in Bethlehem. In early Christian feasts, the Epiphany marked different events in the life of Jesus that revealed Him to the world as the Divine Savior.

The Baptism of Jesus, now celebrated on the Sunday after Epiphany and as read in the Gospel of Mark, revealed Him through His Father's voice as Jesus, His Son.

The Wedding at Cana, now celebrated the Sunday after the Baptism and as read in the Gospel of John, revealed Jesus' "glory" as He performed His first miracle, the changing of the water into wine. Lastly, as we celebrate Epiphany today at the end of the twelve days of Christmas with the Visit of the Magi and as read in the Gospel of Matthew, the Wise Men traveled to pay homage to the newborn baby and revealed Jesus as "King" to the Gentiles.

Traditionally these foreigners came from the East and brought gifts of gold, frankincense and myrrh, symbolic of Jesus as King and as Priest and as Healer.

18

Because of the number of gifts, many believe that there were three kings and they have commonly become known as Melchior, Gaspar and Balthasar. Following the star, they arrived and knelt or prostrated themselves before the Child demonstrating great respect for the newborn King.

The visit from the Magi reveals God the Son as a human in the person of Jesus Christ.

On Epiphany, we celebrate His manifestation to the world as the Son of God.

The Flight into Egypt

Herod, seeing the Magi did not return to him, became very angry, and, resolving to destroy this new-born King, ordered all the children in Bethlehem and the country round about to be put to death.

He foolishly thought Jesus would surely be killed among the rest, little dreaming how easily God could shield Him.

While Herod was preparing for the murder the holy innocents, an angel appeared to Joseph in his sleep, and told him to take the child and its mother and flee into Egypt, and to remain there until told to return.

Without a word of complaint, Joseph rose, and taking the child and its mother, went into Egypt.

He had scarce gone, when Herod's messengers came to Bethlehem, and, tearing the children from their mothers' arms, murdered them.

Every house was filled with lamentation and sorrow, and the prophecy of Jeremiah was fulfilled:

"Rachel bewailing her children, and would not be comforted, because they were not."

As a punishment for his cruelty, Herod died, some years after, amid the horrid torments.

Again the angel appeared to Joseph, and commanded him to return to Judea, because Herod was dead.

Joseph rose, and taking the child and Mary, returned, and dwelled in Nazareth.

Thus it came to pass that Christ was called a Nazarene.

Jesus, the Savior of the world, was saved by a miracle; so was Moses, the savior of the Israelites, saved by a miracle.

The Presentation of Jesus in the Temple

Presentation Prayer

Almighty and Everlasting God,
we humbly beseech Thy Majesty
that as They only-begotten Son
was this day presented in the temple
in the substance of our flesh,
so too Thou wouldst grant us
to be presented unto Thee
with purified souls
and bring us into your presence.
Through the same
Christ our Lord.
Amen

The Presentation of Jesus in the Temple

The Presentation of Jesus in the Temple celebrates the day when Mary and Joseph traveled to Jerusalem to take Jesus to the Temple to present Him to the Lord.

Also known as the Purification of the Virgin, in accordance to the Law of Moses, Mary had to complete her ritual purification forty days after she gave birth and they had to offer the sacrifice of a turtledove or a pigeon if the family could not afford a lamb. A devout prophet named Simeon greeted them in the Temple area.

He had been told that he would not see death until he had seen the Messiah.

He took Jesus in his arms and pronounced that he could now go in peace.

Simeon blessed Jesus and said, "Behold, this child is destined for the fall and rise of many in Israel."

Also in the Temple was a prophetess named Anna who worshipped with prayer and fasting, day and night, never leaving.

She spoke about Jesus to all who would listen and all who were "awaiting the redemption of Jerusalem".

Many refer to this day as Candlemas Day, the day when all of the candles for the church, which must be beeswax, are blessed for the year.

A procession follows representing the entrance of Jesus, the Light of the World, into the Temple. The Feast of the Presentation of Jesus in the Temple is celebrated February 2, or the Sunday between January 28 and February 3 and is the fourth Joyful Mystery of the Rosary.

The Finding of Jesus in the Temple

Prayer of Finding Jesus

To find Jesus through
the fruit of the Holy Spirit
Heavenly Father we pray
that we live our lives
in conformity with the Gospel,
and since we are temples
of your Holy Spirit,
we pray that you help us
to find you as we practice virtue
and aspire to be holy.
May we discover you as we live
with patience, faith, hope, love,
humility, meekness, charity, peace,
generosity, faithfulness and self control.
Amen

The Finding of Jesus in the Temple

The Finding of Jesus in the Temple is the celebration of Mary and Joseph discovering their Son preaching in the Temple area after He had been lost for three days. Mary and Joseph traveled to Jerusalem on Pilgrimage for the Feast of the Passover when Jesus was twelve years old.

The Gospel of Luke explains that as they were all leaving to return home, Jesus stayed behind but his parents thought He was with the rest of the group. After a day of traveling, they looked for Him and could not find Him anywhere.

They returned to Jerusalem and after three days found Him in the Temple speaking with the teachers, asking questions and giving answers far beyond His years. When His parents found Him they asked Him why He stayed in the Temple, separating from the group and worrying His parents. The Gospel tells us that Mary and Joseph were anxious about their Son and Mary asked, "Son, why have you done this to us?" Jesus explained that He must be in His Father's house, doing the work of His Father. This incident gives the only glimpse into the young life of Jesus.

Jesus is dedicated to the mission of the Father but He realizes at this time that Mary and Joseph cannot fully understand what His life must be like to do His Father's work.

So, in obedience to Mary and Joseph, Jesus returns with them to Nazareth and grows in wisdom and favor with God and man. The Finding of Jesus in the Temple is the fifth Joyful Mystery of the Rosary.

The Wedding at Cana

Prayer of the Wedding at Cana

Lord Jesus Christ,
at the wedding feast of Cana,
Mary your mother told
the servants to do as you instructed.
Mary knew the great embarrassment
that would fall upon the newly wedded
couple should there be no wine.
Moved with pity,
she asked you to intercede, and you did.
We pray that we will have the gift of
loving service in our lives as Mary did.
May the compassion
and love of Mary be a witness to
us, and may we imitate that love and
compassion to all we meet.
Amen.

The Wedding at Cana

The Wedding at Cana is the event that leads to Jesus' first miracle in the Gospel of John. Jesus, His disciples and His mother attended a wedding at Cana in Galilee and Mary suddenly discovered that the bridegroom was running out of wine.

She told Jesus knowing that, like her, He would not want to see the host made to feel uncomfortable and dishonored. Jesus questioned His role in the situation and explained, "My hour has not yet come." He spoke of His hour.

Jesus knew that if He took care of the problem, others would know of His Divinity before the time was right.

But His mother worried about the host of the party and told the servants to do whatever Jesus told them to do.

The servants filled the jars with water as Jesus instructed and they took the first taste to the head waiter who complimented the bridegroom for saving the best wine until last. Jesus gives in abundance.

The jars are not only filled to the brim but the wine is also the best of the entire feast.

And, after all is settled, His disciples, we are told, start to believe in Him. Jesus reveals Himself as the Divine Savior.

This first miracle is a sign that makes known His glory. His presence at the Wedding Feast serves as a sign of the importance He puts on the Sacrament of Marriage. The Wedding at Cana is the second Luminous Mystery of the Rosary.

The Baptism of Christ

Prayer of Christ's Baptism

Almighty God,
you anointed Jesus at His baptism
with the Holy Spirit,
and revealed Him
as Your beloved Son;
grant that we who are baptised
into His name
may give up our lives to Your service,
and be found worthy of our calling;
through Jesus Christ our Lord
who is alive with You
in the unity of the Holy Spirit,
one God now and for ever.
Amen.

Baptism of Christ

The Gospels of Matthew, Mark and Luke tell of the Baptism of Jesus which marks the beginning of his public ministry and the decline of the ministry of John the Baptist.

John preached of the kingdom of Heaven and baptized for the forgiveness of sins. He fasted in the desert and wore rough clothes as signs of repentance.

He remained prayerful and contemplative. Many followed him and his preaching. He prepared the way for Jesus.

He preached that One more powerful than Him would come and would baptize with the Holy Spirit.

When Jesus does come to the Jordan to be baptized, John hesitates because he feels Jesus should be the one who baptizes him. "I am the one who has a need to be baptized by you and yet you come to me." But Jesus explains, "it is proper for us to fulfill all righteousness."

Jesus does not come to confess His sinfulness for as we know He was born without sin. Jesus comes to fulfill what is pleasing to God.

He comes to share in our humanity and to give us, by example, the means by which we may be saved. As Jesus is baptized, the heavens open and the Holy Spirit descends as a dove and lands upon Him. We read in the Gospel of Matthew, that a voice from heaven says, "This is my Beloved Son in whom I am well pleased."

The Baptism of Jesus is celebrated on the Sunday following the Epiphany and is the first Luminous Mystery of the Rosary.

The Transfiguration

Transfiguration Prayer

O God,
Who in the glorious transfiguration
of Your only-begotten Son
strengthened the sacraments of faith
by the testimony of the fathers,
and Who wonderfully foreshowed
the perfect adoption of Your children by a
voice coming down
in a shining cloud,
mercifully grant that we be made
co-heirs of the King of glory Himself,
and grant us to be sharers
in that very glory.
Through the same Lord Jesus Christ,
Your Son, Who lives and reigns
with You in the unity of the
Holy Spirit, God,
world without end.
Amen.

The Transfiguration

The Transfiguration of Jesus is told to us in the Gospels of Matthew, Mark and Luke. About a week after Jesus' first prediction of His passion and death, He took Peter, James and John up a high mountain alone away from the other disciples and the crowds of followers. Jesus is transfigured before them.

He is transformed into someone divine or glorified. This helps His disciples to better understand who He really is as they move toward His passion and death.

He is described as having a face that shone like the sun with clothes as white as light.

Moses and Elijah "appeared in glory" and speak to Him of His "exodus" that will occur in Jerusalem. Here Jesus reveals His glory.

The disciples are terrified and Peter offers to make tents for the three of them. Then, suddenly the voice from above says, "This is my beloved Son, with whom I am well pleased; listen to Him." Jesus now is the One to listen to over the Old Testament prophets. Moses and Elijah likely symbolize the old Law and the Prophets which give way to the new.

St. Thomas Aquinas explains that the Transfiguration shows us the Trinity; "the Father in the voice, the Son in the man Jesus and the Spirit in the shining cloud."

The disciples fall with their faces down in fear but Jesus comes to them. When the disciples get up, there is no one there but Jesus.

In the Transfiguration, Jesus gives His disciples a taste of His Glory. It is believed to have taken place on Mount Tabor.

The Transfiguration is the fourth Luminous Mystery of the Rosary.

The Last Supper

Last Supper Prayer

Almighty Father,
whose dear Son,
on the night before he suffered,
instituted the Sacrament
of His Body and Blood:
Mercifully grant that we may receive it
thankfully in remembrance of
Jesus Christ our Lord,
who in these holy mysteries gives us
a pledge of eternal life;
and who now lives and reigns
with You and the Holy Spirit,
one God, forever and ever.
Amen.

The Sacrifice of Christ at the Mass

The Mass was instituted by Christ, the night before He died, at the Last Supper. He took the bread and blessed it. Then, He broke the bread and gave it to His disciples saying, "Take and eat; this is my Body."

Then He took the cup filled with wine, offered thanks and gave it to His disciples saying, "Drink from it, all of you, for this is my Blood of the covenant, which will be shed on behalf of many for the forgiveness of sins."

The Sacrifice Christ makes of Himself for our sins begins here at this table and ends on the cross at Calvarly. This sacrifice is the surrendering of Christ on the cross to His Heavenly Father.

During the Consecration at Mass, Jesus Christ, our High Priest, offers Himself through the priest in commemoration of His death at Calvary.

The bread and wine are changed in the Body and the Blood of Christ. He offers Himself in the Mass as He offered Himself on Calvary, to save us as sinners, that we may one day receive what He won for us on the Cross, Eternal Life.

As the priest stands before the altar of sacrifice and raised the bread and the wine in Consecration, Jesus is offered, in what the Catechism of the Catholic Church defers to as, an "unbloody manner" and we are called to join in this sacrifice.

Our participation in the Sacrifice of the Mass helps to repair our souls from the damage cased by our sins, in the celebration of the Mass throughout the world every day, Jesus offers us the fullness of His mercy and His grace.

The Crucifixion

Prayer to Jesus Crucified

Behold, O kind and most sweet Jesus, I cast; myself upon my knees in Your sight, and with the most fervent desire of my soul, I pray and beseech You that You would impress upon my heart lively sentiments of faith, hope and charity with true contrition for my sins and firm purpose of amendment; while with deep affection and grief of soul I ponder within myself and mentally comtemplate Your five wounds, having before my eyes the words which David the propheat put on Your lips concerning You; "They have pierced my hands and my feet, they have numbered all my bones" (Ps. XXI 17,18).

(Indulgence, 10 years; Plenary once a day, under usual conditions.)

The Crucifixion

The Crucifixion of Jesus is described in all four of the Gospels, Jesus is arrested and taken to the Sanhedrin where He is stripped and spit upon and mocked before He is taken to Pilate. Pilate thinks he may get out of the entire ordeal by offering to release Jesus or Barabbas, known for murder and rebellion.

However, when the two are brought before the people, the crowd chooses to release Barabbas and crucify Jesus. The soldiers take Him to the preatorium where He is stripped and beaten and mocked and crowned with thorns.

They lead Him off and on the way find a Cyrenian named Simon to help Him carry the cross to Golgatha, the Place of the Skull, for His crucifixion. They give Him a wine mixture to drink but He refuses. They nail His hands and His feet to the huge cross, crucifying Him along two criminals, one on His right and one on His left.

They cast lots and divided His clothes and a sign is put on the cross that reads, "The King of the Jews". Those who pass by mock Him calling for Him to save Himself and come down from the cross.

Even one of the criminals hanging next to Him asks Him to save them all, as the other criminal asks simply to be remembered when He enters into His Kingdom. From noon until three in the afternoon, the sky remain dark.

Jesus cries out, "My God, My God, Why Have You Forsaken Me?" Some people hear Him and one runs to get a sponge and soaks it in the wine to get Him to drink. Jesus cries out and takes His last breathe. A centurion facing Jesus says, "Truly this was the Son of God!"

MYSTERIA
DOLOROSA

Prayer to the Holy Cross
(Feast, Sept. 14)

Hail, O Holy Cross,
my light and my strength!
bond of my redemption,
my salvation and my glory.
Hail, O Holy Cross,
my refuge and my shelter!
Hail, emblem of grace,
consolation of the afflicted, impregnable wall
against the power of the evil spirit!
Hail, standard of peace,
adorned by the Blood of Jesus,
and ornamented by His Sacred Limbs
as though by precious stones!
O Holy Cross, You through whom
we have obtained eternal glory,
be my victor over all adverse powers,
the remedy for all my ills,
my support in my weariness,
and the guarantee of the resurrection of my
body. May Jesus, the God-Man, our Saviour,
Who shed His Blood for us,
protect me through You
and conduct me to my heavenly home.
Amen.

The Stations
of the Cross

*This devotion arose first in Jerusalem among
the Christians who dwelt there out of veneration
for those sacred spots which were sanctified
by the sufferings of our Divine Redeemer.
From the Holy City this devout exercise
was introduced into Europe.
When, in 1342, the Franciscan Fathers
established their house in Jerusalem, and undertook
the custody of the sacred places of the Holy Land,
they began to spread throughout the Catholic world
the devotion of the Way of the Cross.
This excellent devotion has been repeatedly
approved by the Holy See, and is enriched
with many Indulgences; to gain them,
it is necessary to meditate,
according to one's ability,
on the Passion and Death of our Lord Jesus Christ,
and to go from one Station to another,
if the space and number of persons will admit.*

PREPARATION

Composed by St.Alphonse Liguori

Let each one, kneeling before the High Altar,
make an act of contrition
and form the intention of
gaining the Indulgences
whether for themself or for
the souls in Purgatory.
Then say:

My Lord Jesus Christ, You have made this
journey to die for me with love unutterable,
and I have so many times
unworthily abandoned You,
but now I love You with my whole heart,
and because I love You,
I repent sincerely for ever having offended You.
Pardon me, my God, and permit me
to accompany You on this journey.
You go to die for love of me; I wish also,
my beloved Redeemer, to die for love of You.
My Jesus, I will live and die always united to You.

STABAT MATER

At the Cross her station keeping,
Stood the mournful Mother weeping,
Close to Jesus to the last.

Pilate said to them,
"Then what am I to do with Jesus, the so-called Messiah?"
"Crucify him!", they all cried.
He said, "Why, what has he committed?."
But they only shouted the louder, "crucify him!."
At that, he released Barabbas to them.
Jesus, however, he first had scourged;
then he handed him over to be crucified.
Mt 27: 22-23,26

THE FIRST STATION
Jesus is Condemned to Death

V. We adore You, O Christ, and we bless You.
R. Because by Your Holy Cross, You have
   redeemed the world.

Priest: *Consider how Jesus, after having been scourged and crowned with thorns, was unjustly condemned by Pilate to die on the Cross.*

People: My adorable Jesus, it was not Pilate, no it was my sins that condemned You to die. I beseech You, by the merits of this sorrowful journey, to assist my soul in its journey towards eternity. I love You, my beloved Jesus; I repent with my whole heart for having offended You. Never permit me to separate myself from You again. Grant that I may love You always; and then do with me what You will.

Our Father, Hail Mary, Glory be to the Father, etc.

STABAT MATER

Through her heart, His sorrow sharing,
All His bitter anguish bearing,
Now at length the sword had passed!

*Afterward they took hold of the reed
and kept striking him on the head.
Finally, when they had finished
making a fool of him, they stripped him
of the cloak, dressed him in his own clothes,
and led him off to crucifixion.*
Mt 27: 30-31

THE SECOND STATION
Jesus Carries His Cross

V. We adore You, O Christ, and we bless You.
R. Because by Your Holy Cross, You have
   redeemed the world.

Priest: *Consider how Jesus, in making this
journey with the Cross on His shoulders thought of
us, and for us offered to His Father the death He was
about to undergo.*

People: My most beloved Jesus, I embrace all
the tribulations You have destined for me until
death. I beseech You, by the merits of the pain
You did suffer in carrying Your Cross, to give
me the necessary help to carry mine with perfect
patience and resignation. I love You, Jesus my
love; I repent for having offended You.
Never permit me to separate myself from
You again. Grant that I may love You always;
and then do with me what You will.

Our Father, Hail Mary, Glory be to the Father, etc.

STABAT MATER

O how sad and sore distressed,
Was that Mother highly blessed
Of the sole-begotten One.

III

Yet it was our infirmities that He bore, our sufferings that He endured, while we thought of him as stricken, as one smitten by God and afflicted.
But he was pierced for our offenses, crushed for our sins; Upon him was the chastisement that makes us whole, by his stripes we were healed.
We had all gone astray like sheep, each following his own way; But the Lord laid upon him the guilt of us all.
Is 53: 4-6

The Third Station

Jesus Falls the First Time

V. We adore You, O Christ, and we bless You.
R. Because by Your Holy Cross, You have
   redeemed the world.

Priest: *Consider this first fall of Jesus under His Cross. His flesh was torn by the scourges, His head crowned with thorns, and He had lost a great quantity of blood. He was so weakened that he could scarcely walk, and yet he had to carry this great load upon His shoulders. The soldiers struck Him rudely, and thus He fell several times in His journey.*

People: My beloved Jesus, it is not the weight of the Cross, but my sins, which have made You suffer so much pain. Ah, by the merits of this first fall, deliver me from the misfortune of falling into mortal sin. I love You, O my Jesus, with my whole heart; I repent for having offended You. Never permit me to separate myself from You again. Grant that I may love You always; and then do with me what You will.

Our Father, Hail Mary, Glory be to the Father, etc.

STABAT MATER

Christ above in torment hangs,
She beneath beholds the pangs
Of her dying, glorious Son.

IV

Simeon blessed them and said to Mary His mother:
"This child is destined to be the downfall and the rise
of many in Israel, a sign that will be opposed,
and you yourself shall be pierced with a sword,
so that the thoughts of many hearts may be laid bare"...
His mother meanwhile pondered all
these things in her heart.
Lk 2: 34-35, 51

The Fourth Station

Jesus Meets His Sorrowful Mother

V. We adore You, O Christ, and we bless You.
R. Because by Your Holy Cross, You have
  redeemed the world.

Priest: *Consider the meeting of the Son and the Mother, which took place on this journey. Jesus and Mary looked at each other, and their looks became as so many arrows to wound those hearts which loved each other so tenderly.*

People: My most loving Jesus, by the sorrow You experienced in this meeting, grant me the grace of a truly devoted love for Your most Holy Mother. And You, my Queen, who was overwhelmed with sorrow, obtain for me by your intercession a continual and tender remembrance of the Passion of Your Son. I love You, Jesus my love; I repent for ever having offended You. Never permit me to offend You again. Grant that I may love You always; and then do with me what You will.

Our Father, Hail Mary, Glory be to the Father, etc.

STABAT MATER

Is there one who would not weep,
Whelmed in miseries so deep,
Christ's dear Mother to behold?

V

As they led him away,
they laid hold of one Simon the Cyrenian
who was coming in from the fields.
They put a crossbeam on Simon's shoulder
for him to carry along behind Jesus.
A great crowd of people followed him,
including women who beat their breasts
and lamented over him.
Lk 23: 26-27

THE FIFTH STATION
Simon Helps Jesus to Carry the Cross

V. We adore You, O Christ, and we bless You.
R. Because by Your Holy Cross, You have
   redeemed the world.

Priest: *Consider how the Jews, seeing that at each step
Jesus took was weakening Him to the point of expiring, and
fearing that He would die on the way, when they wished
Him to die the ignominious death of the Cross, constrained
Simon the Cyrenian to carry the Cross behind our Lord.*

People: **My most sweet Jesus, I will not refuse
the Cross, as the Cyrenian did; I accept it; I embrace
it. I accept in particular the death You have destined
for me; with all the pains that may accompany it; I
unite it to Your death, I offer it to You. You have
died for love of me; I will die for love of You, and
to please You. Help me by Your grace. I love You,
Jesus my love; I repent for having offended You.
Never permit me to offend You again. Grant that
I may love You always; and then do with me what
You will.**

Our Father, Hail Mary, Glory be to the Father, etc.

STABAT MATER

Can the human heart refrain
From partaking in her pain
In that Mother's pain untold.

VI

There was in him no stately bearing
to make us look at him,
nor appearance that would attract us to him.
He was spurned and avoided by men,
a man of suffering, accustomed to infirmity,
One of those from whom men hide their faces.
Is 53: 2-3

THE SIXTH STATION
Veronica Wipes the Face of Jesus

V. We adore You, O Christ, and we bless You.
R. Because by Your Holy Cross, You have
   redeemed the world.

Priest: *Consider how the holy woman named Veronica,
seeing Jesus so afflicted, and His face bathed in sweat and
blood, presented Him with a towel, with which He wiped
His adorable face, leaving on it the impression of His holy
countenance.*

People: My most beloved Jesus, Your face was beautiful
before, but in this journey it has lost all its beauty, and
wounds and blood have disfigured it. Alas, my soul
also was once beautiful, when it received Your grace in
Baptism, but I have disfigured it since by my sins. You
alone, my Redeemer, can restore it to its former beauty.
Do this by Your Passion, O Jesus. I repent for having
offended You. Never permit me to offend You again.
Grant that I may love You always; and then do with me
what You will.

Our Father, Hail Mary, Glory be to the Father, etc.

STABAT MATER

Bruised, derided, cursed, defiled,
She beheld her tender Child,
All with bloody scourges rent.

VII

I am a man who knows affliction from the rod of his
anger, one whom he has led and forced to walk
in darkness, not in the light… He has blocked my ways
with fitted stones, and turned my paths aside…
He has broken my teeth with gravel,
pressed my face in the dust.
Lam 3: 1-2, 9, 16

THE SEVENTH STATION
Jesus Falls the Second Time

V. We adore You, O Christ, and we bless You.
R. Because by Your Holy Cross, You have
   redeemed the world.

Priest: *Consider the second fall of Jesus under the Cross a fall which renews the pain of all the wounds of the head and members of our afflicted Lord.*

People: My most gentle Jesus, how many times You have pardoned me, and how many times have I fallen again, and begun again to offend You. Oh, by the merits of this new fall, give me the necessary help to persevere in Your grace until death. Grant that in all temptations which assail me I may always commend myself to You. I love You, Jesus my love; I repent for having offended You. Never permit me to offend You again. Grant that I may love You always; and then do with me what You will.

Our Father, Hail Mary, Glory be to the Father, etc.

STABAT MATER

For the sins of His own nation
Saw Him hang in desolation
Till His spirit forth He sent.

VIII

Jesus turned to them and said:
Daughters of Jerusalem, do not weep for me.
Weep for yourselves and for your children,
The days are coming when they will say, 'Happy are the
sterile, the wombs that never bore, and the breasts that
never nursed'. Then they will begin saying to the mountains,
'Fall on us', and to the hills, 'Cover us'. If they do these
things in the green wood, what will happen in the dry?
Lk 23: 28-31

THE EIGHTH STATION

The Women of Jerusalem Weep over Jesus

V. We adore You, O Christ, and we bless You
R. Because by Your Holy Cross, You have
   redeemed the world.

Priest: Consider how those women wept with compassion at seeing Jesus in such a pitiable state, streaming with blood, as He walked along. But Jesus said to them: Weep not for Me, but for your children.

People: My Jesus, laden with sorrows, I weep for the offences I have committed against You, because of the pains they have deserved, and still more because of the displeasure they have caused You, who has loved me so much. It is Your love, more than the fear of hell, which causes me to weep for my sins. My Jesus, I love You more than myself; I repent for having offended You. Never permit me to offend You again. Grant that I may love You always; and then do with me what You will.

Our Father, Hail Mary, Glory be to the Father, etc.

STABAT MATER

O thou Mother! Font of love,
Touch my spirit from above,
Make my heart with Yours accord

IX

It is for a man to bear the yoke from his youth.
Let him sit alone and in silence, when it is laid upon him.
Let him put his mouth to the dust; there may yet be hope.
Let him offer his cheek to be struck, let him be filled with
disgrace. For the Lord's rejection does not last forever;
Though he punishes, he takes pity,
in the abundance of his mercies.
Lam 3: 27-32

THE NINTH STATION
Jesus Falls the Third Time

V. We adore You, O Christ, and we bless You
R. Because by Your Holy Cross, You have
   redeemed the world.

*Priest: Consider the third fall of Jesus Christ. His
weakness was extreme, and the cruelty of His executioners
was excessive, who tried to hasten His steps when He had
scarcely strength to move.*

People: Ah, my outraged Jesus, by the merits of the
weakness You did suffer in going to Calvary, give me
strength sufficient to conquer all human respect, and
all my wicked passions, which have led me to despise
Your friendship. I love You, Jesus my love, with my
whole heart; I repent for having offended You. Never
permit me to offend You again. Grant that I may love
You always; and then do with me what You will.

Our Father, Hail Mary, Glory be to the Father, etc.

STABAT MATER

Make me feel as You have felt;
Make my soul to glow and melt
With the love of Christ my Lord

X

Upon arriving at a site called Golgotha,
a name which means Skull Place, they gave him a drink
of wine flavored with gall, which he tasted but refused
to drink. When they had crucified him,
they divided his clothes among them by casting lots;
then they sat down there and kept watch over him.
Mt 27: 33-36

THE TENTH STATION

Jesus is Stripped of His Garments

V. We adore You, O Christ, and we bless You.
R. Because by Your Holy Cross, You have
   redeemed the world.

Priest: *Consider the violence with which the executioners
stripped Jesus. His inner garments adhered to His torn flesh,
and they dragged them off so roughly that the skin came with
them. Compassionate your Savior that was cruelly treated,
and say to Him:*

People: My innocent Jesus, by the merits of the
torment You felt, help me to strip myself of all
affection to things of earth, in order that I may place
all my love in You, who are so worthy of my love. I
love You, O Jesus, with my whole heart; I repent for
having offended You. Never permit me to offend You
again. Grant that I may love You always; and then do
with me what You will.

Our Father, Hail Mary, Glory be to the Father, etc.

STABAT MATER

Holy Mother! pierce me through,
In my heart each wound renew
Of my Savior crucified.

XI

It was about nine in the morning when they crucified
him. The inscription proclaiming his offence read:
"The King of the Jews."
With him they crucified two insurgents,
one at his right and one at his left.
Mk 15: 25-27

THE ELEVENTH STATION

Jesus is Nailed to the Cross

V. We adore You, O Christ, and we bless You.
R. Because by Your Holy Cross, You have
   redeemed the world.

Priest: Consider how Jesus, after being thrown on the Cross extended His hands, and offered to His Eternal Father the sacrifice of His death for our salvation. These barbarians fastened Him with nails, and then, raising the Cross, allowed Him to die with anguish on this infamous gibbet.

People: My Jesus! Loaded with contempt, nail my heart to Your feet, that it may ever remain there, to love You, and never quit You again. I love You more than myself; I repent for having offended You. Never permit me to offend You again. Grant that I may love You always; and then do with me what You will.

Our Father, Hail Mary, Glory be to the Father, etc.

STABAT MATER

Let me share with You His pain,
Who for all my sins was slain,
Who for me in torment died.

XII

From noon onward, there was darkness over the whole land until midafternoon. Then toward midafternnon Jesus cried out in a loud tone, "Eli, Eli, lema sabachthani?." That is, "My God, my God, why have you forsaken me?." This made some of the bystanders who heard it remark, "He is invoking Elijah!" Once again Jesus cried out in a loud voice, and then gave up his spirit.

Mt 27: 45-47, 50

The Twelfth Station

Jesus is Raised upon the Cross, and Dies

V. We adore You, O Christ, and we bless You.
R. Because by Your Holy Cross, You have
   redeemed the world.

Priest: *Consider how Jesus, after three hours Agony on the Cross, consumed at length with anguish, abandons Himself to the weight of His body, bows His head, and dies.*

People: O my dying Jesus, I kiss devoutly the Cross on which You died for love of me. I have merited by my sins to die a miserable death; but Your death is my hope. Ah, by the merits of Your death, give me grace to die, embracing Your feet, and burning with love for You. I yield my soul into Your hands. I love You with my whole heart; I repent for ever having offended You. Never permit me to offend You again. Grant that I may love You always; and then do with me what You will.

Our Father, Hail Mary, Glory be to the Father, etc.

STABAT MATER

Let me mingle tears with thee,
Mourning Him who mourned for me,
All the days that I may live.

XIII

The centurion and his men who were keeping watch
over Jesus were terror-stricken at seeing the earthquake
and all that was happening, and said: "Clearly this was
the Son of God!." Many women were present looking
on from a distance. They had followed Jesus from
Galilee to attend to his needs.
Mt 27: 54-55

THE THIRTEENTH STATION

Jesus is Taken Down from the Cross

V. We adore You, O Christ, and we bless You.
R. Because by Your Holy Cross, You have
   redeemed the world.

Priest: *Consider how, after the death of our Lord, two of His disciples, Joseph and Nicodemus, took Him down from the Cross, and placed Him in the arms of His afflicted Mother, who received Him with unutterable tenderness, and pressed Him to her bosom.*

People: O Mother of sorrow, for the love of Your Son, accept me as Your servant, and pray to Him for me. And You, my Redeemer, since You have died for me, permit me to love You; for I wish for You, and nothing more. I love You, my Jesus, and I repent for ever having offended You. Never permit me to offend You again. Grant that I may love You always; and then do with me what You will.

Our Father, Hail Mary, Glory be to the Father, etc.

STABAT MATER

By the cross with You to stay;
There with You to weep and pray,
Is all I ask of You to give.

XIV

When evening fell, a wealthy man from Arimathea arrived,
Joseph by name. He was another of Jesus' disciples,
and had gone to request the body of Jesus.
There upon Pilate issued an order for its release.
Taking the body, Joseph wrapped it in fresh linen and laid it
in his own new tomb which had been hewn from a formation
of rock. Then he rolled a huge stone across
the entrance of the tomb and went away.

Mt 27: 57-60

THE FOURTEENTH STATION
Jesus is Laid in the Sepulchre

V. We adore You, O Christ, and we bless You.
R. Because by Your Holy Cross, You have
    redeemed the world.

Priest: Consider how the disciples carried the body of Jesus to bury it, accompanied by His holy Mother, who arranged it in the sepulchre with her own hands. They then closed the tomb, and all withdrew.

People: Oh, my buried Jesus, I kiss the stone that encloses You. But You rose again on the third day. I beseech You, by Your resurrection, make me rise gloriously with You on the last day, to be always united with You in heaven, to praise You and love You forever. I love You, and I repent for ever having offended You. Never permit me to offend You again. Grant that I may love You always; and then do with me what You will.

Our Father, Hail Mary, Glory be to the Father, etc.

STABAT MATER

Virgin of all Virgins best!
Listen to my fond request;
Let me share your grief divine.

Crucifixion Prayer

O adorable Lord and Saviour Jesus Christ, Dying on the gallows tree for our sins, O Holy Cross of Jesus see me in my thoughts, O Holy Cross of Christ ward off from me all weapons of danger. O Holy Cross of Christ, ward off from me things that are evil. O Holy Cross of Christ protect me from my enemies. O Holy Cross of Christ, ward off from me all dangerous deaths; give always life.

O Crucified Jesus of Nazareth have mercy on me now and forever. In honor of our Lord Jesus Christ and in the honor of His Sacred Passion, and in the honor of His Holy Resurrection and God Jesus Christ and in the like ascension, He likes to bring me right to Heaven.

True as Jesus Christ was born on Christmas day in the Stables, true as Jesus

Christ was crucified on Mount Calvary on Good Friday, true as the three wise kings brought their offerings on the thirteenth day, true as He ascended into Heaven, so the Honor of Jesus will keep me from enemies visible and invisible now and forever more.

O Lord Jesus Christ, have mercy. Joseph, who took our Lord down from the cross and buried Him, O Lord Jesus Christ through Your sufferings, for truly, Your soul was parting out of this sinful world. Give Grace that I may carry my cross patiently with dread and fear when I suffer, and without complaining, and that through Your suffering I may escape all danger now and for evermore. Amen.

The Five Wounds

St. Gertrude's Salutation of the Five Wounds of our Savior

Hail, most precious wounds of Jesus, in the omnipotence of the Father, Who decreed you; hail, in the wisdom of the Son, Who endured you; hail, in the goodness of the Holy Spirit Who through you accomplished the work of human redemption. To you I commend myself, into you I plunge myself, that in your shelter I may be secure from the destroyer. Amen.

Prayers of St. Clare of Assisi to the Five Wounds of Our Savior

1. To the Wound in the Right Hand

Praise be to You, O Jesus Christ, for the most sacred wound in Your right hand. By this adorable wound, and by Your most sacred Passion, pardon me all the sins I have committed against You in thought, word, and deed, and all negligence in Your service, and all sensuality for which I have been to blame whether asleep or awake. Grant that I may be able to recall with devotion Your most sorrowful death and sacred wounds; grant me the grace to mortify my body, and so to offer a pledge of my gratitude to You. Who lives and reigns forever and ever. Amen.

Our Father, Hail Mary, etc.

2. To the Wound in the Left Hand

Praise and Glory be to You, O amiable Jesus Christ, for the most sacred wound in Your left hand. By this adorable wound, have mercy on me, and deign to root out of my heart everything displeasing to You. Give me victory over Your perverse enemies, so that with Your grace I may be able to overcome them; and by the merits of Your most sorrowful death save me from all the dangers of my present and future life. And then grant that I may share Your glory in heaven. Who lives and reigns forever and ever. Amen.

Our Father, Hail Mary, etc.

3. To the Wound in the Right Foot

Praise and glory be to You, O patient Jesus Christ, for the most sacred wound in Your right foot; and by that adorable wound grant me grace to do penance for my sins. By Your most sorrowful death I devoutly beg of You to keep me, Your poor servant, united night and day to Your Holy Will, and to remove afar off every misfortune of body and soul. And when the day of wrath comes, receive me into Your mercy, and lead me to eternal happiness. Who lives and reigns forever and ever. Amen.

Our Father, Hail Mary, etc.

4. To the Wound in the Left Foot

Praise and glory be to You, O adorable Jesus Christ, for the most sacred wound in Your left foot; and by this adorable wound grant me the grace of a full pardon, that with Your aid I may deserve to escape the sentence of eternal condemnaton. I implore You, moreover, by Your most holy death, O my loving Redeemer, that I may be able before my death to receive the Sacrament of Your Body and Blood, after confession of my sins, and with perfect repentance and purity of body and mind. Grant that I may merit also to receive the holy anointing for my eternal salvation, O Lord, Who lives and reigns forever and ever. Amen.

Our Father, Hail Mary, etc.

5. To the Wound in the Sacred Side

Praise and glory be to You, O loving Jesus Christ, for the most sacred wound in Your side, and by that adorable wound, and by Your infinite mercy, which You made known in the opening of Your breast to the soldier Longinus, and so to us all, I implore You, O most gentle Jesus, that having redeemed me by baptism from original sin, so now by Your Precious Blood, which is offered and received throughout the world, deliver me from all evils, past, present, and to come. And by Your most bitter death give me a lively faith, a firm hope, and a perfect charity, so that I may love You with all my heart, and all my soul, and all my strength; make me firm and steadfast in good works, and grant me perseverance in Your service, so that I may be able to please You always. Amen.

Our Father, Hail Mary, etc.

V. We adore You, O Christ, and we bless You.

R. Because by Your death and Blood You have redeemed the world.

LET US PRAY

Almighty and everlasting God,
Who by the five wounds of Your Son,
our Lord Jesus Christ,
has redeemed the human race,
grant to Your followers that
we who daily venerate those wounds, may, by the
shedding of His Precious Blood,
be freed from sudden and everlasting death.
Through the same Christ our Lord.
Amen

Novena to the Holy Face

O Lord Jesus Christ, in presenting ourselves before Thine adorable Face, to ask of Thee the graces of which we stand in most need, we beseech Thee above all, to grant us that interior disposition of never refusing at any time to what Thou requires of us by Thy holy commandments and divine inspirations. Amen.

O Good Jesus, who hadst said, "Ask and you shall receive, seek and ye shall find, knock and it shall be open to you," grant us O lord, that faith which obtains all, or supply in us what may be deficient; grant us, by the pure effect of Thy charity, and for Thine eternal glory, the graces which we need and which we look from Thine infinite mercy. Amen.

Be merciful to us., O my God, and reject not our prayers, when amid our afflictions, we call upon Thy Holy Name and seek with love and confidence Thine Adorable Face. Amen.

O Almighty and Eternal God, look upon the Face of Thy Son Jesus. We present it to Thee with confidence to implore Thy pardon. The all-Merciful Advocate opens His mouth to plead our cause; hearken to His cries, behold His tears, O God, and through His infinite merits, hearken to Him when He intercedes for us poor miserable sinners. Amen.

Adorable Face of Jesus, my only love, my light, and my life, grant that I may know Thee, love Thee and serve Thee alone, that I may live with Thee, of Thee, by Thee and for Thee. Amen.

Eternal Father, I offer Thee the adorable Face of Thy Beloved Son for the honor and glory of Thy Name, for the conversion of sinners and the salvation of the dying. O Divine Jesus, through Thy Face and Name, save us. Our Hope is in the virtue of Thy Holy Name! Amen.

VERONICA'S VEIL
as preserved in Rome

HOLY FACE PRAYER

Eternal Father, we offer You the Holy Face of Jesus, covered with blood, sweat, dust and spit, in reparation for the crimes of atheists, blasphemers, and for the profaners of the Holy Name and of the Holy Day of Sunday. Amen.

St. Therese and the Holy Face

St. Therese of Lisieux, the "Little Flower", was known in religious life as "Sister Therese of the Child Jesus and the Holy Face".

O Jesus, who in Thy bitter Passion didst become "the most abject of men, a man of sorrows", I venerate Thy Sacred Face whereon there once did shine the beauty and sweetness of the Godhead; but now it has become for me as if it were the face of a leper! Nevertheless, under those disfigured features, I recognize Thy infinite Love and I am consumed with the desire to love Thee and make Thee loved by all men.

The tears which well up abundantly in Thy sacred eyes appear to me as so many precious pearls that I love to gather up, in order to purchase the souls of poor sinners by means of their infinite value. O Jesus, whose adorable face ravishes my heart, I implore Thee to fix deep within me Thy divine image and to set me on fire with Thy Love, that I may be found worthy to come to the contemplation of Thy glorious Face in Heaven. Amen.

Veronica with Christ's Holy Veil

ACT OF REPARATION TO THE HOLY FACE

I adore and praise You, O my divine Jesus, Son of the living God, and I desire to make satisfaction for all the outrages which I, the most miserable of Your creatures, have offered You in all the members of Your Blessed Body, and particularity in Your adorable Face.

Hail, worshipful face, disfigured by spit, and hardly to be recognized through the cruel treatment which You received from the impious Jews.

I salute You, O blessed eyes, all bathed in tears, which You shed for our salvation.

I salute You, O blessed ears, assailed by blasphemies, insults, and cruel mockeries.

I salute You, O blessed mouth, filled with graces and tenderness for poor sinners, but embittered with vinegar and gall by the monstrous ingratitude of that people whom You chose from among all others. In reparation for all these ignominies I offer You all the homage which is given You in that holy place where You are pleased to be honored with a special worship, uniting myself therewith.

The Resurrection

The Resurrection Prayer

God our Father,
by raising Christ Your Son
you conquered the power of death
and opened for us the way
to eternal life.
Let our celebration today raise us up and
renew our lives by the Spirit
that is within us.
Grant this through our
Lord Jesus Christ, Your Son,
who lives and reigns with You
and the Holy Spirit, one God,
for ever and ever.
Amen.

The Resurrection

The Resurrection of Jesus is the rising from death to life of Jesus three days after His crucifixion. Each of the four Gospels share accounts of the Resurrection.

In his Gospel, Mark recounts that Mary Magdelene, Mary mother of James and Salome go to the tomb to anoint Jesus' body with spices. Upon their arrival, the stone is rolled away and the tomb is found empty.

Each Gospel passage has a slightly different referral to an angel who tells the women not to be afraid because He has risen from the dead just as He said He would. They run to tell His disciples and Peter rushes ahead to the tomb to see for himself. Jesus meets Mary Magdelene on the road and tells her not to be afraid and not to keep holding onto Him. She leaves to tell the disciples that she has seen Jesus and He is Alive.

The Resurrection is Jesus' victory over death. His was not simply a "bringing back" to life but a rising to a new life that would never again experience death. He is the perfect example of obedience to His Father. Because of the Resurrection, life does not end in death.

Jesus' rising from death to new life opens for us the opportunity for Eternal Life.

With His Passion, Death and Glorification, the Resurrection of Jesus is part of the Paschal Mystery which we celebrate in the Sacrament of the Eucharist. The celebration of the Resurrection is Easter Sunday. The Resurrection of Jesus is the First Glorious Mystery of the Rosary.

RESURRECTION NOVENA

Jesus, I believe that by Your own power, You rose from death, as You promised, a glorious Victor.

May this mystery strengthen my hope in another and better life after death, the resurrection of my body on the last day, and an eternity of happiness.

I firmly hope that You will keep Your promise to me and raise me up glorified. Though Your glorious resurrection I hope that You will make my body like Your own in glory and life, and permit me to dwell with You in Heaven for all eternity. I believe that Your resurrection is the crown of Your life and work as God-Man, because it is Your glorification.

This is the beginning of the glorious life that was due to You as the Son of God. Your resurrection is also the reward of Your life of suffering.

Jesus, my risen Lord and King, I adore Your Sacred Humanity which receives this eternal Kingdom of honor, power, joy and glory. I rejoice with You, my Master, glorious, immortal and all-powerful. Through the glorious mystery of Your resurrection, I ask You to help me to rise with You spiritually and to live a life free from sin, that I may be bent upon doing God's Will in all things, and may be patient in suffering. Through the Sacraments may my soul be enriched evermore with sanctifying grace, the source of Divine life. I also ask that You grant me this special request... (mention silently your special intentions). May Your Will be done!

Jesus Appears to His Disciples

Prayer for Jesus Appearing to His Disciples

On the eighth day after
Your resurrection, You , O Lord,
came to Your disciples,
although the doors were closed,
and bestow the gifts of
the Holy Spirit upon them.
And then You said
to Your disciple Thomas,
"Come here and touch Me!" and he, at
the touch, knew You as being truly risen
and not an apparition.
He, then together with the other
disciples did he cry unto You: Alleluia.

Jesus Appears to His Disciples

After His Resurrection, Jesus appears to the disciples when Thomas is not present. They have been told by Mary of Magdala that He has risen but when He enters the room although the doors are locked and they see His hands and His side, then they truly rejoice.

He gives them the gift of the Holy Spirit and through the Spirit the gift to forgive or retain the sins of those who ask forgiveness; the sacrament of reconciliation.

The disciples are called to go forth and to bring others to the Father just as Jesus has done.

They are excited over seeing the Risen Christ and upon finding Thomas they tell him of the appearance of Jesus.

Thomas will not believe them and comments that he would have to actually put his finger in the nail marks and his hand in His side.

A week later Jesus appears again to the disciples and with Thomas present He approaches and tells him to put his finger in the nail marks and his hand in His side.

Jesus wants Thomas to believe. Thomas responds, "My Lord and my God".

(A traditional though not required response in the Latin Mass when the host was elevated at the consecration) And, the Gospel of John continues to explain that these stories are written so that we may ourselves believe in Jesus the Risen Christ, the Son of God, and that because of our belief, we may have "life in His name".

Jesus considers us blessed who believe in Him even though we cannot see Him.

The Apostles, including Thomas, believe and are sent forth on their mission to bring others to have faith and to believe in the Risen Lord.

The Supper at Emmaus

Prayer of the Supper at Emmaus

O God,
whose blessed Son
did manifest himself
to his disciples
in the breaking of bread;
Open, we pray thee,
the eyes of our faith,
that we may behold thee
in all thy works;
through the same
thy Son Jesus Christ our Lord.
Amen.

The Way to Emmaus

he encounter between Jesus and two of His disciples on the Road to Emmaus is told in the Gospel of Luke. After the Resurrection of Jesus, two disciples are walking to the village, Emmaus, and talking about all that has happened.

As they walk, Jesus joins them but they do not recognize Him. He asks them what they are discussing and they stop, not believing that this man has not heard all that has been happening in Jerusalem. Cleopas and the other disciple, whose name is not revealed, explain that Jesus of Nazareth had been a great prophet and the chief priests and leaders handed Him over to be condemned to death and crucified.

They explain their hope that He was their redeemer; possibly they mean the one who would free Israel from Roman occupation but as we know, He is the One who brings salvation; who conquers sin and death. We understand that the two disciples have been told that women from their group were at the tomb in the morning and did not find Jesus, but instead found a vision of angels telling of His Resurrection.

After He listens to the two men, Jesus then begins to unravel the Scriptures beginning with Moses and the prophets, interpreting everything about Himself.

As they approach Emmaus, Jesus walks ahead but the two men ask Him to stay with them. When they eat, as Jesus blesses and give thanks and breaks the bread and hands it to them, they recognize Him.

"Then their eyes were opened..." As quickly as He had joined them, Jesus leaves but they continue to talk about how they were attracted to Him as He opened the Scriptures to them along the Road to Emmaus.

"Were not our hearts burning within us...?" They later find the other disciples and tell them all that had happened to them along the way.

The Ascension

The Ascension Prayer

O Christ,
You ascended in glory
on the Mount of Olives
in the presence
of Your disciples.

O You who penetrate all things
with Your divinity,
You were enthroned
at the right hand of Your Father
and sent down upon Your disciples
the Holy Spirit who enlightens,
strengthens, and saves our souls.
Amen.

The Ascension

The Ascension of Jesus is the rising of Jesus into Heaven forty days after His Resurrection from the dead.

The Ascension story is found in the Gospels of Mark and Luke and in the Acts of the Apostles. In the Gospel of Mark, after commissioning the eleven apostles, Jesus is taken up into Heaven and seated at the right hand of the Father.

In the Gospel of Luke, after He appears to the apostles and opens their minds to understand and preach the Scriptures, He leads them out to Bethany.

He blesses them and then is taken up to Heaven. In the Acts of the Apostles, He speaks to them about being His witnesses then He is lifted up and a cloud takes Him. Two men appear and ask why they are looking up at the sky and tell them He will return in the same way.

The Ascension of Jesus, included in both the Apostle's Creed and the Nicene Creed, is a central element in our Christian tradition. We believe Jesus rose from the dead and ascended into Heaven and sits at the right hand of the Father.

Jesus goes before us. He leads the way so that we may live in the hope of one day being with Him in Heaven.

He sends His Holy Spirit to guide us. In His humanity, He reigns in glory.

He prepares a place for us and intercedes for us to the Father.

We celebrate the Ascension forty days after Easter Sunday. The Ascension of Jesus is the second Glorious Mystery of the Rosary.

Prayer to the Precious Blood

O Sacred Blood, that flowed so copiously seven times for my salvation, I love You, I praise You, I adore You with the deepest feeling of gratitude! The purest fountain from which You did flow makes Your memory so sweet.

O Precious Blood, with trumpet tones You speak to me of the love of my God and Redeemer. How I deplore my coldness and indifference towards You! Now, at last, I wish to return love for love, blood for blood, if necesssary.

As often as my pulse beats, it shall greet You.

You sweet guest of my soul, and shall return to the arteries warmed and purified by Your love. As long as the blood courses through my veins, it shall flow only for love of You; it shall turn cold and stand still only because I am about to love You in eternity.

Oh, let this stream of Your love flow through every heart and inebriate it with holy joy!

My dearest Mother Mary, I beseech you with confidence, obtain for me, although your unworthy child, the blessing of God the Father, by covering me with the merits of your Son Jesus, that I may regain my eternal birthright in Heaven.

Clothe me every evening, Sweet Lady of Mt. Carmel, but especially on the eve of my life, with the "Dyed Garments" of the Precious Blood.

Amen.

NOVENA TO
THE PRECIOUS BLOOD!

By the voice of Your Blood, O Jesus, we would press You, solicit You, importune You. Though You seem to reject our supplications, we will not leave Your bleeding feet until You hear our prayers. So many graces, so many mercies have come forth from Your Blood that we shall not cease to hope even to the end, in its efficacy. Then, O Jesus, by Your precious Blood seven times shed for the welfare of men, by each drop of that Sacred Price of our Redemption, by the tears of Your Immaculate Mother, we entreat You to hear our prays.

(Here pause and mention your requests)

O You, Who during all the days of Your mortal life consoled so many sufferings, healed so many infirmities, encourages so many who were disheartened, You will not fail to have pity on a soul who cries to You from the depths of her anguish! No, it is impossible. Another sigh from our wounded hearts and from the wounds in Your own will flow to us upon a wave of Thy Precious Blood The graces we ardently desire! O Jesus, hasten the moment when You will change our tears into joys, our sighs into thanksgivings.

Holy Mary, source of the Divine Blood, we entreat you not to lose this occasion for glorifying the Blood which made you immaculate.

Amen.

THE LITANY OF THE MOST PRECIOUS BLOOD

Lord,	*have mercy on us.*
Christ,	*have mercy on us.*
Lord,	*have mercy on us.*
Christ,	*hear us.*
Christ,	*graciously hear us.*
God, the Father of heaven,	*Have mercy on us.*
God, the Son, Redeemer of the world,	*Have mercy on us.*
God, the Holy Spirit,	*Have mercy on us.*
Holy Trinity, One God,	*Have mercy on us.*

Blood of Christ,
only begotten Son of the Eternal Father, *Save us.*

Blood of Christ,
Incarnate Word of God, *Save us.*

Blood of Christ,
of the New and Eternal Testament, *Save us.*

Blood of Christ,
falling upon the earth in the Agony, *Save us.*

Blood of Christ,
shed profusely in the Scourging, *Save us.*

Blood of Christ,
flowing forth in the Crowning with Thorns, *Save us.*

Blood of Christ,
poured out on the Cross, *Save us.*

Blood of Christ,
price of our salvation, *Save us.*

Blood of Christ,
without which there is no forgiveness, *Save us.*

Blood of Christ,
Eucharistic drink and refreshment of souls, *Save us.*

Blood of Christ,
stream of mercy, *Save us.*

Blood of Chirst, victor over demons,	*Save us.*
Blood of Christ, courage of martyrs,	*Save us.*
Blood of Christ, strength of confessors,	*Save us.*
Blood of Christ, bringing forth virgins,	*Save us.*
Blood of Christ, help of those in peril,	*Save us.*
Blood of Christ, relief of the burdened,	*Save us.*
Blood of Christ, solace in sorrow,	*Save us.*
Blood of Christ, hope of the penitent,	*Save us.*
Blood of Christ, consolation of the dying,	*Save us.*
Blood of Christ, peace and tenderness of hearts,	*Save us.*
Blood of Christ, pledge of Eternal Life,	*Save us.*
Blood of Christ, freeing souls from Purgatory,	*Save us.*
Blood of Christ,	
most worthy of all glory and honor,	*Save us.*

Lamb of God, You take away the sins of the world,
Spare us, O Lord.
Lamb of God, You take away the sins of the world,
Graciously hear us, O Lord.
Lamb of God, You take away the sins of the world,
Have mercy on us.

V. You have redeemed us, O Lord, in Your Blood.
R. And made us, for our God, a kingdom.

LET US PRAY

Almighty and Eternal God, You appointed Your only-begotten Son the Redeemer of the world, and willed to be appeased by His Blood.

Grant, we beg of You, that we may worthily adore this price of our salvation, and through its power be safeguarded from the evils of this present life, so that we may rejoice in its fruits forever in heaven.

Through the same Jesus Christ our Lord.
Amen.

Sacred Heart of Jesus

Prayer to the Sacred Heart of Jesus

O Sacred Heart of Jesus,
filled with Infinite Love;
broken by our ingratitude
and pierced by our sins;
yet loving us still;
accept the consecration
we make to Thee of all that
we are and all that we have.
Take every faculty of our souls
and bodies, only day by day
draw us nearer and nearer to
Thy Sacred Heart; and there
as we shall hear the lesson,
teach us Thy Holy Way

I will Bless Every Place Where
A Picture Of My Heart Shall Be
Exposed And Honored.

Sacred Heart of Jesus

The Sacred Heart of Jesus is a special form of devotion to the physical heart of Jesus. It is the love He shares with the Father and the Holy Spirit for humanity.

In the eleventh and twelfth centuries, devotion to the Sacred Heart arose in Benedictine and Cistercian monasteries.

Passages from the published work "Vitis Mystica" inspired the devotion and were used by the Church for the lessons of the Second Nocturn of the feast.

From the thirteenth to the sixteenth centuries the devotion was practiced by different congregations such as Franciscans, Dominicans and Carthusians but remained an individual or private devotion. St. Eudes made the devotion public in the seventeenth century, gave it an Office and established a feast for it.

He shared devotion to the Sacred Heart with his devotion to the Immaculate Heart. Little by little the devotions separated and the first feast of the Sacred Heart of Jesus was celebrated on August 31, 1670.

On December 27, 1673, on the Feast of St. John, St. Margaret Mary Alacoque, a sister at the Visitation Convent in France, began to have visions of Jesus. He asked her to promote devotion to his heart, symbolic of His love for humanity.

Jesus attached twelve promises to those who practiced devotion to His Sacred Heart including peace in families, consolation in time of trouble, abundant blessings and refuge at the hour of death.

By order of Pope Leo XIII in 1899, all mankind was solemnly consecrated to the Sacred Heart.

Jesus' Sacred Heart is typically pictured as a flaming heart, pierced, surrounded by a crown of thorns and bleeding.

The wounds and thorns symbolize the manner of His death and the fire represents His burning, undying love.

THE PRAYER OF THE SACRED HEART OF JESUS

O God, who in the heart of Thy Son,
wounded by our sins,
did deign mercifully to bestow upon us
the infinite treasures of Thy love,
grant, we beseech You,
that we who now pay Him
the devout homage of our piety,
may also perform the duty
of worthy satisfaction.
Through the same Jesus Christ,
Our Lord, who lives and reigns
with the unity of the Holy Spirit,
God, world without end.
Amen.

NOVENA OF THE SACRED HEART OF JESUS

First Day

The word heart is a strong word and a beautiful one. "Take heart!" we say, when we want a man to pick up courage.

"He gave her his heart", we say, when a man gives to a woman his pure love.

With perfect understanding we talk of a motherly heart... of a man who puts heart into his work... of the innocent heart of a child ... of the pulsing heart of a city.

What more natural then that when Christ the Savior revealed Himself once more to humanity He should borrow our word, knowing that it would ring with complete familiarity?

"Behold the heart that hath loved men so much," He cried, indicating His own heart. And men of good heart and of loving heart answered, "Indeed we know how much you have loved us."

To the Savior who revealed Himself to the word that needs love, we say:

The Prayer of the
Sacred Heart of Jesus
(recite prayer on page 122)

Second Day

Ours is a gracious God of love, of that there is no slightest doubt.

God the Father created the world lovingly and tenderly. The long passages of the ages – a flash of God's eternity – were spent in the preparation of a beautiful, convenient, well-stocked earth to be man's dwelling place.

The newly made creatures, made to the image and likeness of the heavenly Father, He adopted as His sons and daughters.

When in dark rebellion these sons and daughters revolted, "God so loved the world, as to give His only-begotten Son that... the world may be saved..."

The love story of God is written anew in the star of Bethlehem, the smile of the Child Jesus, His hidden life of service to Mary and to the villagers of Nazareth, the miracles and parables of His public life, the death by which Christ laid down His life for His friends.

Then on the wings of wind and in the symbolic form of flame the Spirit of love came to dwell in human souls, divine love taking up its residence in the men and the women that God had loved into life, loved unto death, loved to their own sanctification.

Before the three Persons of the Trinity, who love us with a divine love, we kneel and pray:

The Prayer of the
Sacred Heart of Jesus
(recite prayer on page 122)

Third Day

Christ of the tender and loving heart...

The Infant heart that beat with the impulse of love on Christmas...

The heart that yearned over the world, which was dark in ignorance and wandering in sin..

The heart that leaped in response to the love of Mary and knew the warmth of a devoted Son for the foster father who guarded Him tenderly...

The heart that could hardly wait for the beginnings of His work among men...

The heart that wept over the lost multitudes...

The heart of the Good Shepherd searching for His lost sheep.

The heart that speaks in the poetry of the parables and the strength of the sermons...

The heart that yearned for sinners and drove the Savior questing for them far into the night...

The heart that raised the widow's son from death.

The heart that selected twelve men as intimate friends and then responded gratefully to the love of the innocent John...

The heart that poured itself out in miracles of healing and forgiveness and mercy and loving kindness...

This is the Sacred Heart of the historic Savior. To this heart we say:

The Prayer of the
Sacred Heart of Jesus
(recite prayer on page 122)

127

Fourth Day

The heart of the Savior broke during the course of the Passion.

The paschal moon that shone with fierce brilliance over the garden was like a searchlight beating upon the sins of the parading world. Christ saw that world, knew its horror and vileness, and broke into a bloody sweat.

Yet that heart held Him captive when the traitor came and made Him call the betrayer friend.

Upon the loving Savior, bound, not with cords and chains, but by His heartstrings, fell the blows of the scourging, the mockery of the mob, the spittle of the soldiers, the awful humiliation of public rejection. It was His heart rather than His head that was crowned with thorns.

Upon the cross it was His heart that held Him fast. He loved us and delivered Himself for us.

He bore our bruises and our infirmities.

Greater love than this no man hath, that He die for His executioners. And that the last drop of love might flow out and the lowest and meanest of His sinners might find safe entrance to His heart.

He offers that heart to the lance of the centurion. In the cleft of His heart, as in the cleft of a rock, the penitent world has found warmth, safety, and protection. Before the suffering Christ of love we say:

The Prayer of the
Sacred Heart of Jesus
(recite prayer on page 122)

Fifth Day

The ages roll swiftly along their course.

God's love for His creatures is undying.

The love of Christ lives on in the Mass and in the sacraments and in His abiding presence upon the altar and in the soul.

But men are fickle. Doubt is a cold and chilling thing. The hot flame of passion has a way of dying down to the dark, cold, dusty ashes of bitterness and despair.

So it was that into an age when men taught the denial of God's love, when they rejected His presence on the altar or forbade believers to approach the altar, the God of love came again.

A little nun, holy and loving, knelt in her Visitation Convent. Margaret Mary, she was called. The combination of the two names has become music to the Catholic world ever since that time.

On the altar before her was the vision of the loving Christ.

There was shown the tortured, flaming heart.

There were spoken such words of pathetic beauty, of such divine yearning, of dignity combined with passion that only God could have said them.

"Behold the heart that has loved men so much and has been loved so little in return."

Beholding that heart, we kneel adoringly to say:

*The Prayer of the
Sacred Heart of Jesus
(recite prayer on page 122)*

Sixth Day

As the symbol of love, Christ had chosen the heart, the favorite symbol of human speech.

It was His human heart, still pierced with the spear of Calvary, still open to welcome returning sinners.

Around that heart was twined the crown of thorns; for though Christ is indeed king, He is a king who won His kingdom along the bloody course of love.

From the heart leap up living flames. They are like the tongues that descended upon the Apostles when the Spirit of love came to inflame them for the apostolate. These flames are restless, as love is always restless; but while, like fire, they warm and light, they do not burn or destroy or even smudge.

A tiny cross, that unfailing symbol of God's love even unto death, surmounts the heart.

Poetry has known that a sequence of sonnets could not say what a single glimpse of this heart reveals.

Catholics everywhere have looked upon the heart of the Savior and have known that it was offered to them. God's heart was theirs for the asking, theirs if only they would give their own worthless hearts in exchange.

Before the symbol of the Sacred Heart we say:

The Prayer of the
Sacred Heart of Jesus
(recite prayer on page 122)

CONGREGAVIT NOS IN UNUM CHRISTI AMOR

Seventh Day

Love is always generous. It gives without the prospect of reward. It asks only to give in a flooding desire to be lavishly generous.

Much as the heart of the Savior had during His public life sought love and responded to love and been divinely grateful for the slightest sign of love, that heart always thought first in terms of giving... giving...and more giving...

Miracles for the needy, forgiveness for the sinful, faith for those in darkness, hope for the despairful - these were the outpourings of the heart of the Savior.

Now again He speaks, this time to promise the sweet gifts of His love.

To those who love Him, assurance of eternal salvation...

To those who honor a picture of Him, peace in their households and blessings upon their family.

His reward for little acts of devotion just before death... His presence in the Blessed Sacrament...

Favors, gifts — promises made out of the greatness of His love — to anyone who will show some little signs of love for Him...

With that vision the great devotion to the Sacred Heart of Jesus, old as Christianity itself but new in its present manifestation, moves in the wind-fed fire of love across the earth.

Loving the lover of our souls, we say:

The Prayer of the
Sacred Heart of Jesus
(recite prayer on page 122)

Eighth Day

"Behold the heart that has loved men so much and that has been loved so little in return."

It is upon the second half of the Savior's statement that the loving Christian focuses his attention.

We have known always the love of God. We have tried not to remember the lovelessness of men and women.

With love for everyone and for everything, now as on the first Christmas, no love remains for Christ. With love walking in a thousand cheap disguises, as it did even during the climax of love on Calvary, love passes by without a nod to the victim of love.

That is why the Savior Himself asked loving souls for a little reparation.

"Make up", He pleads, "for the millions who do not love me."

"Tell me at least that you wish sinners would stop their sin, and the faithful in name would become faithful in fact, and the sins committed in the ugly travesty on love would cease to kill the human power of love."

"Consecrate yourself", He begs, "to my heart. Dedicate your homes and your children to my loving protection. Spend at least an occasional hour with me." We consecrate ourselves to the loving Christ and say:

The Prayer of the
Sacred Heart of Jesus
(recite prayer on page 122)

Ninth Day

Christ of the Sacred Heart, Christ of the Blessed Sacrament – these two are identical. Devotion to the Sacred Heart is inseparably linked to devotion to the Holy Eucharist. Love for the Sacred Heart must inevitably lead to the tabernacle.

Host and heart are equally manifestations of the love of the Savior for saints and sinners.

The impulse of love in the heart of the Savior made inevitable the promise of the Eucharist, which climaxed the love feast of the loaves and the fishes. Love in the wonderful evening before His Passion, when love was the sole subject of His speech, inevitably passed beyond words and became bread made flesh and wine made blood with the guarantee that never would He leave us orphans.

That is why in His revelation to Saint Margaret Mary, Christ speaks of Holy Communion, that close union of the human soul with the divine. That is why He asks that on the first Friday we come to welcome Him. That is why He begs that on our knees before His loving presence in the tabernacle we find the historic Christ in the Eucharistic Christ and remember that the love of Christ is the same yesterday, today, and forever.

Before the Eucharistic heart of Christ we kneel and say:

The Prayer of the
Sacred Heart of Jesus
(recite prayer on page 122)

PROMISES OF THE
SACRED HEART OF JESUS

Of the many promises Our Lord Jesus Christ did reveal to Saint Margaret Mary in favor of souls devoted to His Sacred Heart the principal ones are as follows:

1. I will give them all the graces necessary for their state of life.

2. I will give peace in their families.

3. I will console them in all their troubles.

4. I will be their refuge in life and especially in death.

5. I will abundantly bless all their undertakings.

6. Sinners shall find in my Heart the source and infinite ocean of mercy.

7. Tepid souls shall become fervent.

8. Fervent souls shall rise speedily to great perfection.

9. I will bless those places wherein the image of My Sacred Heart shall be exposed and venerated.

10. I will give to priests the power to touch the most hardened hearts.

11. Persons who propagate this devotion shall have their names eternally written in my Heart.

12. In the excess of the mercy of my Heart, I promise you that my all powerful love will grant to all those who will receive Communion on the First Friday for nine consecutive months, the grace of final repentance: they will not die in my displeasure, nor without receiving the Sacraments; and my Heart will be their secure refuge in that last hour.

O Sacred Heart of Jesus, I Place My Trust in Thee

O Sacred Heart of Jesus,
I place my trust in Thee,
Whatever may befall me, Lord,
though dark the hour may be;
In all my woes, in all my joys,
though naught but grief I see,
O Sacred Heart of Jesus,
I place my trust in Thee.
When those I loved have passed away,
and I am sore distressed,
O Sacred Heart of Jesus,
I fly to Thee for rest.
In all my trials, great or small,
my confidence shall be Unshaken
as I cry, dear Lord,
I place my trust in Thee.
This is my one sweet prayer, dear Lord,
My faith, my trust, my love,
But most of all in that last hour,
when death points up above,
O sweet Savior, may Thy face
smile on my soul all free;
Oh may I cry with rapturous love:
"I've placed my trust in Thee!"

Consecration to the Sacred Heart of Jesus

*Merciful Jesus,
I consecrate myself today and always
to Your Most Sacred Heart.*

*Most Sacred Heart of Jesus
I implore, that I may ever
love You more and more.*

*Most Sacred Heart of Jesus
I trust in You!
Most Sacred Heart of Jesus
have mercy on us!*

*Most Sacred Heart of Jesus
I believe in Your love for me.*

*Jesus, meek and humble of heart,
make my heart like Your Heart.
Amen.*

ACT OF REPARATION TO THE SACRED HEART OF JESUS

O sweet Jesus, Whose overflowing charity for men is requited by so much forgetfulness, negligence and contempt, behold us prostrate before Your altar eager to repair by a special act of homage the cruel indifference and injuries, to which Your loving Heart is everywhere subject. Mindful alas! That we ourselves have had a share in such great indignities, which we now deplore from the depths of our hearts, we humbly ask Your pardon and declare our readiness to atone by voluntary expiation not only for our own personal offenses, but also for the sins of those, who, straying far from the path of salvation, refuse in their obstinate infidelity to follow You, their Shepherd and Leader, or, renouncing the vows of their baptism, have cast off the sweet yoke of Your Law.

We are now resolved to expiate each and every deplorable outrage committed against You; we are determined to make amends for the manifold offenses against Christian modesty in unbecoming dress and behavior, for all the foul seductions laid to ensnare the feet of the innocent, for the frequent violation of Sundays and holidays, and the shocking blasphemies uttered against You and Your Saints. We wish also to make amends for the insults to which Your Vicar on earth and Your priests are subjected, for the profanation, by conscious neglect of terrible acts of sacrilege, of the very Sacrament of Your divine love; and lastly for the public crimes of nations who resist the rights and the teaching authority of the Church which You have founded. Would, O divine Jesus, we were able to wash away such abominations with our blood. We now offer, in reparation for these violations of Your divine honor, the satisfaction You once made to Your eternal Father on the cross and which You continue to renew daily on our altars; we offer it in union with the acts of atonement of Your Virgin Mother and all the Saints and the pious faithful on earth; and we sincerely promise to make recompense, as far as we can with the help of Your grace, for all neglect of Your great love and for the sins we and others have committed in the past. Henceforth we will live a life of unwavering faith, of purity of conduct, of perfect observance of the precepts of the gospel and especially that of charity. We promise to the best of our power to prevent others from offending You and to bring as many as possible to follow You.

O loving Jesus, through the intercession of the Blessed Virgin Mary, our model in reparation, deign to receive the voluntary offering we make of this act of expiation; and by the crowning gift of perseverance keep us faithful unto death in our duty and the allegiance we owe to You, so that we may all one day come to that happy home, where You with the Father and the Holy Spirit lives and reigns, God, world without end. Amen.

LITANY TO THE SACRED HEART

Lord, have mercy.
Lord, have mercy on us,
Christ, hear us,
God the Father of Heaven,
God the Son,
    Redeemer of the world,
God the Holy Spirit,
Holy Trinity, one God,
Heart of Jesus,
Son of the Eternal Father,
Heart of Jesus,
formed by the Holy Spirit in
the womb of the Virgin Mother,
Heart of Jesus,
one with the eternal Word,
Heart of Jesus,
infinite in majesty,
Heart of Jesus,
holy temple of God,
Heart of Jesus,
tabernacle of the Most High,
Heart of Jesus,
house of God and gate of heaven,
Heart of Jesus,
aflame with love for us,
Heart of Jesus,
source of justice and love,
Heart of Jesus,
full of goodness and love,
Heart of Jesus,
wellspring of all virtue,
Heart of Jesus,
worthy of all praise
Heart of Jesus,
king and center of all hearts,
Heart of Jesus,
treasure house of wisdom
and knowledge,

Christ, have mercy.
Christ, have mercy.
Christ, graciously hear us.
have mercy on us.

have mercy on us.
have mercy on us.
have mercy on us.
"
"

"

"

"

"

"

"

"

"

"

"

"

"

Heart of Jesus,
in whom there dwells
the fullness of God,   have mercy on us.
Heart of Jesus,
in whom the Father is well pleased,   "
Heart of Jesus,
from whose fullness
we have all received,   "
Heart of Jesus,
desire of the eternal hills,   "
Heart of Jesus,
patient and full of mercy,   "
Heart of Jesus,
generous to all who turn to You,   "
Heart of Jesus,
fountain of life and holiness,   "
Heart of Jesus,
atonement for our sins,   "
Heart of Jesus,
overwhelmed with insults,   "
Heart of Jesus,
broken for our sins,   "
Heart of Jesus,
obedient even to death,   "
Heart of Jesus,
pierced by a lance,   "
Heart of Jesus,
source of all consolation,   "
Heart of Jesus,
our life and resurrection,   "
Heart of Jesus,
victim for our sins   "
Heart of Jesus,
    hope of all who die in You,   "
Heart of Jesus,
    delight of all the saints,
    victim for our sins   "

147

Lamb of God, Who takes away the sins of the world,
Spare us, O Lord.
Lamb of God, Who takes away the sins of the world,
Graciously hear us, O Lord,
Lamb of God, Who takes away the sins of the world,
Have mercy on us.

V. Jesus, gentle and humble of heart.
R. Touch our hearts and make them like Your own.

LET US PRAY

O Almighty and Eternal God look upon the Heart of your dearly beloved Son and upon the praise and satisfaction he offers You in behalf of sinners and being appeased grant pardon to those who seek Your mercy in the name of the same Jesus Christ your Son who lives and reigns with You in the Holy Spirit world without end. Amen.

149

Devotions to the Mysteries of the Sacred Infancy

Incline unto our aid, O God.

R.　O Lord, make haste to help us.

V.　Glory be to the Father, and to the Son, and to the Holy Spirit.

R.　As it was in the beginning, is now and ever shall be, one God, world without end. Amen.

Our Father, etc.

Jesus, sweetest Child, Who coming down from the bosom of the Father for our salvation, did not disdain the womb of the Virgin, where, conceived by the Holy Spirit, You, the Word Incarnate, took upon Yourself the form of a servant, have mercy on us.

Have mercy on us, Child Jesus, have mercy on us. Hail Mary, etc.

Jesus, sweetest Child, Who in Your Virgin Mother's womb visited St. Elizabeth and fill Your precursor, John the Baptist, with the Holy Spirit, sanctifying him from his mother's womb, have mercy on us.

Have mercy on us, Child Jesus, have mercy on us. Hail Mary, etc.

Jesus, sweetest Child, Who for nine months hidden in Your Mother's womb, and awaited with eager expectation by the Virgin Mary and by St. Joseph, was offered by them to God the Father for the salvation of the world, have mercy on us.

Have mercy on us, Child Jesus, have mercy on us. Hail Mary, etc.

Jesus, sweetest Child, born in Bethlehem of the Virgin Mary, wrapped in swaddling-clothes, laid in the manger, heralded by angels, visited by shepherds, have mercy on us.

Have mercy on us, Child Jesus, have mercy on us. Hail Mary, etc.

Jesus, sweetest Child, wounded in the circumcision on the eighth day, called by the glorious Name of Jesus, and by Your Name and by Your Blood, to be the Savior of the world, have mercy on us.

Have mercy on us, Child Jesus, have mercy on us. Hail Mary, etc.

Jesus, Sweetest Child, Who was manifested to the three kings, who worshipped You as You lied on Mary's breast, and offered to You the mysterious presents of gold, frankincense and myrrh, have mercy on us.

Have mercy on us, Child Jesus, have mercy on us. Hail Mary, etc.

Jesus, sweetest Child, presented in the Temple by the Virgin Mary, embraced by the holy old man Simeon, and revealed to the Jews by Anna the prophetess, have mercy on us.

Have mercy on us. Child Jesus, have mercy on us. Hail Mary, etc.

Jesus, sweetest Child, Whom Herod sought to slay, carried by St. Joseph with Your Mother into Egypt, saved from death by flight, and glorified by the blood of the holy innocents, have mercy on us.

Have mercy on us, Child Jesus, have mercy on us. Hail Mary, etc.

> *O Jesus, born of Virgin bright!*
> *Immortal glory be to Thee;*
> *Praise to the Father infinite,*
> *And Holy Ghost, eternally.*

V. Christ is at hand.

R. Come, let us adore Him. Our Father, etc.

Jesus, sweetest Child Who, with Mary most holy and the patriarch St. Joseph, dwelled in Egypt until the death of Herod, have mercy on us.

Have mercy on us, Child Jesus, have mercy on us. Hail Mary, etc.

Jesus, sweetest Child, Who returned with Your parents from Egypt into the land of Israel, Who suffered many toils by the way, and entered the city Nazareth, have mercy on us.

Have mercy on us, Child Jesus, have mercy on us. Hail Mary, etc.

Jesus, sweetest Child, who lived most humbly in the blessed house of Nazareth, subject to Your parents, spending Your life in poverty and toil, and growing in wisdom, in age, and in grace, have mercy on us.

Have mercy on us, Child Jesus, have mercy on us. Hail Mary, etc.

Jesus, sweetest Child, brought to Jerusalem when twelve years old, sought by your parents with much sorrow, and after three days found, to their great joy, among the doctors, have mercy on us.

Have mercy on us, Child Jesus, have mercy on us. Hail Mary, etc.

O Jesus, born of Virgin bright!
Immortal glory be to Thee;
Praise to the Father infinite,
And Holy Ghost, eternally.

P.   The Word was made flesh. Alleluia.
S.   And dwelled among us. Alleluia.

LET US PRAY

Almighty and everlasting God, Lord of heaven and earth, who revealed Yourself to little ones, grant us, we beseech You, reverently to honor the holy mysteries of Your Son, the Child Jesus, and to follow Him humbly in our lives, so that we may come to the eternal kingdom promised by You to little ones. Through the same Christ our Lord. Amen.

Infant Sacred Heart of Jesus

Novena to the Divine Child Jesus

Divine Child Jesus, we believe in You; We adore You; and we love You; have mercy on us, sinners.

We've come to this Temple in response to Your love. We've come in response to your mercy and grace. We are here because You invited us to come before You and to pour out the cares of our hearts to You since You deeply care for each of us.

We remember Your words to the disciples: Ask and you shall receive. Seek and you shall find. Knock and the door shall be opened. Trusting in Your infinite goodness and trusting that You always keep Your promise, we now ask this intention which we pray in the silence of our hearts...<silently mention the request>...

Thank you, Divine Child Jesus, for listening attentively to our prayers all the time. We hope that You will ask this before Our Heavenly Father. And, if what we ask for may not be good for our salvation and sanctification, we trust that You will grant us instead what we truly need, so that one day we may be with You for all eternity enjoying that ultimate happiness of Heaven.

Divine Child Jesus, bless and protect us.

Divine Child Jesus, bless and lead us.

Divine Child Jesus, bless and provide for us.

All this we ask through the intercession of Your Holy Mother, Mary, and in Your powerful and Most Holy Name, Jesus. Amen

Divine Child Jesus

A Salesian priest, Fr. John Del Rizzo, was sent to Bogota, Columbia in the early 1900's to take care of the poor and the sick. He was directed by his Superior to beg for donations to build a Church.

He had difficulty asking the poor people for money and the first day he returned without having collected anything. As he knelt in front of the Blessed Mother to ask her help, he looked intently at the Child Jesus in her arms. He had often asked Mary to intercede for him so he decided this time to go directly to Divino Nino Jesus.

He began praying to the Infant Jesus to help him in his endeavors. A local artisan made a statue of the Child Jesus for him. Fr. John prayed to the Infant every day before he had to ask for money from the people.

A sense of calm came over him from the people. A sense of calm came over him and day after day he brought home the donations from the people.

In 1937, the cornerstone for the Church was blessed. When the Church was finished, large numbers of people came every Sunday.

Fr. John Del Rizzo devoted his life to spreading devotion to the Child Jesus and to caring for the poor people in Columbia.

He died in 1957 but devotion to the Divine Infant grew and in 1992 a Sanctuary was completed to welcome all who visited.

Many, many miracles are said to have taken place there. The original statue depicts the Child dressed in pink with His arms open to receive us.

Here, He offers His heart to the world symbolizing His great love and mercy for all who come to Him.

THE PRAYER OF THE INFANT OF PRAGUE

THE PRAYER OF CHRIST THE KING

Almighty, everlasting God,
Who did will that all things should be
made new in thy beloved Son,
the universal king,
mercifully grant that all
kindred of the Gentiles scattered
by the ravages of sin may be brought
under the sweet yoke of His rule.
Who lives and reigns
with God the Father
in the unity of the Holy Spirit, God,
world without end.
Amen

THE INFANT OF PRAGUE

DEVOTION to the Infant Jesus of Prague is devotion to the Child Jesus. It is veneration of the Son of God, who in the form of an infant chose a stable for a palace, a manger for a cradle, and shepherds for worshippers. Our Savior grants special graces to all who venerate His sacred Infancy.

The image of the Child Jesus known as the "Infant Jesus of Prague" was in reality of Spanish origin. In the 17th century, this beautiful statue was brought by a Spanish princess to Bohemia and presented to a Carmelite monastery.

For many years this statue has been enshrined on a side altar in the Church of Our Lady of Victory in the city of Prague. It is of wax, and is about nineteen inches high. It is clothed in a royal mantle, and has a beautiful jewelled crown on its head.

Its right hand is raised in blessing; its left holds a globe signifying sovereignty.

So many graces have been received by those who invoke the Divine Child before the Original statue that it has been called "The Miraculous Infant Jesus of Prague."

We read the following in an old book printed in Kempt: "All who approach the miraculous statue and pray there with confidence receive assistance in danger, consolation in sorrows, aid in poverty, comfort in anxiety, light in spiritual darkness, streams of grace in dryness of soul, health in sickness, and hope in despair."

In thanksgiving for the numerous graces and cures received, the miraculous statue at Prague was solemnly crowned on the Sunday after Easter, in 1665.

What is said of the original statue may be applied also to the images of the "Little King" which are venerated the world over.

From small beginnings, this devotion has grown to great proportions. The Divine Child attracts an ever-increasing number of clients who appeal to Him in every need.

Novena to the Infant of Prague

First Day

Happily familiar to Catholics the world over is the little Infant of Prague.

The dear and charming statues of Him, copied from the miraculous image in the capital of the Czech Republic, belong now to the whole of Catholicity. Today they can be found almost everywhere.

Christ is a king.

This fact we cerebrate in the majestic and glorious feast of Christ the King.

But Christ is the king not only of power and might. He is the king not alone of terrible love, ruling from His cross, the conquering monarch entering into the glory of His heavenly kingdom.

He is also the Infant King, the king of Bethlehem and of the nursery in Nazareth... the king too small to defend Himself save by flight into Egypt... the king small enough to hide in the Host or in a human breast.

So before the little Infant of Prague we say:

The Prayer of the Infant of Prague,
the Prayer of Christ the King
(recite the prayer on page 159)

Second Day

Fundamental to Christianity and basic to our faith and hope is the fact that the Son of God, the second Person of the Blessed Trinity, became a Baby.

This was the wonder that exalted the early Christians and repelled the pagan monarchs.

Suddenly the best of good news broke over the horizon. The remote God was as near as Bethlehem. The great God had become as small as a baby. The hands that fashioned the universe were infant hands. The all-creative voice that had cried the stupendous "Fiat lux" broke into the cries of babyhood.

"We can pick up our God in our arms and hold Him as we hold a child." The thought made early Christians overjoyed as they took Him as their guest in the Eucharist.

To the pagan world the idea was repellent.

A king must be powerful, aloof, threatening, crowned with awesome majesty.

He must be reached through messengers and surrounded by the restraining pomp of courts.

So God became a Baby. Christianity was born with the birth of an Infant King. Christ's birth was like a rebirth for human souls.

Before the Infant King we say:

The Prayer of the Infant of Prague,
the Prayer of Christ the King
(recite the prayer on page 159)

Third Day

It was given to Wise Men to see the kingship of Infancy.

A million, million Christians have prayerfully and happily followed the Magi as they travelled from pagandom into the very center of Christianity.

Exultantly Catholics have seen these men, the wisest of their times, pierce the thin veil of babyhood and know that a Child could be a king, and God could in His quest of hearts assume the most heart warming disguise. Wise as only the holy are wise, they saw the majesty in humility and the strength in love. Before the Infant King they placed their royal treasures.

How like they were to those holy souls who in far-off Prague placed about the Infant King the trappings of royalty. The three Wise Men gave Him jewels to stud into a crown, and gold to beat into fine thread for His royal raiment, and the perfumes that were burned only in the braziers that sent clouds of sacrificial incense upward to God.

History repeats itself with gay insistence. The gifts that were laid at the feet of the Infant of Bethlehem, modern faith has duplicated for the Infant of Prague.

We join the Magi in saying:

The Prayer of the Infant of Prague,
the Prayer of Christ the King
(recite the prayer on page 159)

Fourth Day

Our age likes to think of itself as wise and grown up and sophisticated. Often we see our age for what it is, old and tired and faltering to an atomic grave. It was the wisest of all teachers, Christ Himself, who reminded us that unless we become as little children we shall not enter the kingdom of heaven.

Nicodemus was puzzled by the whole idea of rebirth, infancy, childhood. Christ explained to him, on that secret night of his abashed visit, the rebirth through baptism. All His life Christ explained to the tired old world of His age the importance of the virtues that keep the world young. Sin makes men old. Virtue keeps them immortally young. Sin speeds us to quick death. Virtue wings us to endless life.

"Suffer the little children to come unto me... for of such is the kingdom of God"... men and women of childlike faith in their Father in heaven... men and women unwearied by the dull pounding of sin... How wise the Church to encourage us, of this weary old generation, to kneel before the holy Infant and learn once more the beauties of childhood and the virtues of a heart that never grows old. Before the young king, the Infant God, we say:

The Prayer of the Infant of Prague,
the Prayer of Christ the King
(recite the prayer on page 159)

Fifth Day

"Unless you... become as little children..."

Who among us does not turn back to the happy days of childhood?

The incredible moment of our first communion...the day when in confirmation we became temples of the Holy Spirit...the years when mother and father were all in all to us and carried every burden and guarded us against all dangers.

Those were days without worry or burden, without the demands of each day pressing hard upon us. The world was new and beautiful, and God was very near. We walked with our guardian angel. We knew the saints by their favorite names.

Sin had not put its lines on our soul.

We loved purely, and we acted on warm, generous impulses.

Why regret childhood? Saints grow old; but they are the happy children of God's tenderest protecting care, whatever their weight of years or mantle of responsibility.

We might ask God to give us back the childhood of our souls, our simple faith, our untarnished love, our clear vision of the supernatural, our trust in our fellow men, our glimpses of heaven all around us. All this we ask of the Infant of Prague in:

The Prayer of the Infant of Prague,
the Prayer of Christ the King
(recite the prayer on page 159)

Sixth Day

In an age that depends upon adult cleverness, it is like God to work miracles before the statue of a little child.

The statue of the Infant of Prague has been a wonder-working statue. In itself it is, as all statues are, stone or plaster or wood. In its symbolism it is deep and precious and meaningful.

So it has been that near the feet of the Baby King the sick have found their health, the troubled their peace, the weary their rest, the doubting their faith, the despairing their hope.

Strangely enough it has been toward temporal affairs, the affairs that are constantly bungled and mismanaged by the wise adults of earth, that the miracles have flowed most frequently.

Why not? God has used the wisdom of the simple to confound the wise, as He used the Babe of Bethlehem to upset the wiles of Herod and brought into ancient Egypt the eternal Word of God, His Infant Son.

Miracles there will always be, but only for the trusting hearts.

In a cynical world, only a humble heart shall be so blessed. So asking for simple faith, which is always the fountain of the greatest miracles, we say:

The Prayer of the Infant of Prague,
the Prayer of Christ the King
(recite the prayer on page 159)

Seventh Day

Before the Infant Christ was born into the world, childhood was not a precious thing.

Life was cheap, and the attitude of the pagan world toward new life was contemptuous.

Only those who were strong enough to enforce their demands had any rights. Then came the Infant Christ, and for the first time childhood became precious. Every baby born into the world by God's hope and design was His child and heir.

Christianity saw in strong, pure, religious youth the guarantee of strong, pure, religious nations. Marriage was founded no longer chiefly upon the lust of man and woman, a love that was to ripen into the living symbol of love-the newborn baby.

The child completed upon earth the trinity of home-itself an incarnate spirit of love-as the Holy Spirit of love completed the Trinity of heaven.

As we look upon the Infant of Prague, we are glad that God became weak so that we could learn tenderness and mercy to the weak. We are glad that the Infant in the holy house gave marriage its high dignity and the home its beautiful sanctity.

Conscious of the dignity of childhood, we say:

The Prayer of the Infant of Prague,
the Prayer of Christ the King
(recite the prayer on page 159)

Eighth Day

Christ is our king; of that there is no doubt.

Though He was battered and broken, He could stand in the presence of Pilate, representative of Rome's powerful monarch, and accept that governor's wondering question about His royalty.

"You say-and rightly-that I am king."

No other king was ever more truly king in his own right than was Christ. As St. John points out in his glorious opening verses, the world is His, for He made it. When He established the unending kingdom of His Church, He took over the world, knowing that that Church would see kingdoms and empires, republics and democracies rise and fall while it went its calm way.

But most important He is king because a million, million men and women have freely and gladly accepted Him. He is the king of hearts, the monarch of souls, the ruler of men's lives, the master of their destinies. He is the sovereign who never disappoints the emperor who walks at the side of His humblest subject.

He who said, "I will be with you all days even to the consummation of the world," has chosen to keep His promise to us in our day in the guise of an infant, if only to confound our worldliness.

Before the Infant King we say:

The Prayer of the Infant of Prague,
the Prayer of Christ the King
(recite the prayer on page 159)

Ninth Day

Christ is our king; of that there is no doubt.

Though He was battered and broken, He could stand in the presence of Pilate, representative of Rome's powerful monarch, and accept that governor's wondering question about His royalty.

"You say-and rightly-that I am king."

No other king was ever more truly king in his own right than was Christ. As St. John points out in his glorious opening verses, the world is His, for He made it. When He established the unending kingdom of His Church, He took over the world, knowing that that Church would see kingdoms and empires, republics and democracies rise and fall while it went its calm way.

But most important He is king because a million, million men and women have freely and gladly accepted Him. He is the king of hearts, the monarch of souls, the ruler of men's lives, the master of their destinies. He is the sovereign who never disappoints the emperor who walks at the side of His humblest subject.

He who said, "I will be with you all days even to the consummation of the world," has chosen to keep His promise to us in our day in the guise of an infant, if only to confound our worldliness.

Before the Infant King we say:

The Prayer of the Infant of Prague,
the Prayer of Christ the King
(recite the prayer on page 159)

"POWERFUL NOVENA OF CHILDLIKE CONFIDENCE"

(This Novena is to be said at the same time every hour for nine consecutive hours - just one day).

O Jesus, Who has said, "Ask and you shall receive, seek and you shall find, knock and it shall be opened," through the intercession of Mary, Your Most Holy Mother, I knock, I seek, I ask that my prayer be granted.

(Make your request)

O Jesus, Who has said, "All that you ask of the Father in My Name, He will grant you," through the intercession of Mary Your Most Holy Mother, I humbly and urgently ask your Father in your name that my prayer will be granted.

(Make your request)

O Jesus, Who has said, "Heaven and earth shall pass away but My word shall not pass away," through the intercession of Mary Your Most Holy Mother, I feel confident that my prayer will be granted.

(Make your request)

Imprimatur: Francis Cardinal Spellman, D.D.
New York January 2, 1942

PRAYER TO THE INFANT OF PRAGUE

BY REV. CYRIL OF THE MOTHER OF GOD

*(the first and most devoted venerator
of the Infant of Prague)*

Infant Jesus, through the intercession of Mary, Your mother, I beg Your help in my needs. I believe that You are all powerful and can protect me. Full of confidence, I come to You, knowing that You will give me graces.

Repenting of my sins and asking You to free me from their fetters, I now give my heart entirely to You. I firmly propose to amend my ways and never offend You again. I resolve to patiently suffer everything for You, so as to serve You eternally. For You I will love my neighbor as myself. I ask You, dear Jesus, to help me in my needs, so that I may enjoy You for all eternity with Mary, Joseph and the angels. Amen.

LITANY OF THE MIRACULOUS INFANT

Lord, have mercy.   Christ, have mercy.
Lord, have mercy on us,   Christ, have mercy.
Christ, hear us,   Christ, graciously hear us.
God the Father of Heaven,   have mercy on us.
God the Son,
Redeemer of the world,   have mercy on us.
God the Holy Spirit,   have mercy on us.

O miraculous Infant Jesus,   have mercy on us.
Infant Jesus, true God and Lord,   "
Infant Jesus, Whose omnipotence is
manifested in a wonderful manner,   "
Infant Jesus, Whose wisdom searches
our hearts and minds,   "
Infant Jesus, Whose goodness
continually inclines to aid us,   "
Infant Jesus, Whose providence leads us
to our last end and destiny,   "
Infant Jesus, Whose truth enlightens
the darkness of our hearts,   "
Infant Jesus, Whose generosity
enriches our poverty,   "
Infant Jesus, Whose friendship
consoles the afflicted,   "
Infant Jesus, Whose mercy
forgives our sins,   "
Infant Jesus, Whose strength
invigorates us,   "
Infant Jesus, Whose power turns
away all evils,   "
Infant Jesus, Whose justice deters
us from sin,   "
Infant Jesus, Whose power
conquers Hell,   "

Infant Jesus, Whose lovely countenance
attracts our hearts,   have mercy on us.
Infant Jesus, Whose greatness holds
the universe in its hand,   "
Infant Jesus, Whose miraculous hand
raised in benediction
fills us with all blessings,   "
Infant Jesus, Whose glory
fills the whole world,   "
Be merciful,   Spare us O Jesus.
Be merciful,   Graciously hear us O Jesus.
From all evil,   Deliver us, O Jesus.
From all sin,   "
From all distrust of
Your infinite goodness,   "
From all doubts in
Your power of miracles,   "
From all lukewarmness in
Your veneration,   "
From all trials and misfortunes,
Through the mysteries of
Your holy Childhood,   "
Through the intercession
of Mary, Your Virgin Mother and   We beseech You
St. Joseph Your foster father,   hear us.
That You would pardon us,   "
That You would bring us
to true repentance,   "
That You would preserve and
increase in us love and devotion to
Your sacred Infancy,   "
That You would never withdraw
Your miraculous hand from us,   "
That You would keep us mindful of
Your numberless benefits,   "
That You would inflame us more
and more with love for
Your Sacred Heart,   "

That You would graciously hear all
who call upon You with confidence,
That You would preserve
our country in peace,
That You would free us from all
impending evils,
That You would give eternal life to
all who act generously toward You,
That You would pronounce a merciful
sentence on us at the judgement,
That You would in Your miraculous
Image remain our consoling refuge,
Jesus, Son of God and of Mary,

We beseech You
hear us.
"
"
"
"
"
"

Lamb of God, Who takes away the sins of the world,
Spare us, O Lord.
Lamb of God, Who takes away the sins of the world,
Graciously hear us, O Lord,
Lamb of God, Who takes away the sins of the world,
Have mercy on us.

V. Infant Jesus, hear us.
R. Infant Jesus, graciously hear us.

LET US PRAY

Divine Jesus, miraculous Infant, kneeling before Your sacred image, we implore You to hear our prayer. You whose tender heart went out to all, You who gave sight to the blind, healed lepers, made the deaf hear and the dumb speak, You who brought the dead back to life, grant us, we beg You, the graces we humbly ask, through Your merits, O Lord, Jesus Christ. Amen

Prayer to the Divine Mercy

O Lord, behold here before You a soul who exists in this world in order to allow You to exercise Your admirable MERCY and manifest it before heaven and earth. Others may glorify You through their faithfulness and perseverance, thus making the power of Your grace. How sweet and generous You are to those who are faithful to You!

Nevertheless, I will glorify You by acquainting others of Your goodness to sinners and by reminding them that Your MERCY is above all malice, that nothing can be exhaust it, and that no relapse, no matter how shameful or criminal, should allow the sinner to despair of forgiveness.

I have offended You grievously, O Beloved Redeemer, but it would be still worse if I were to offend You by thinking that You were lacking in goodness to forgive me. I would rather He deprive me of everything else than the Trust I have in Your Mercy.

Should I fall a hundred times or should my crimes be a hundred times worse that they actually are, I would continue to trust in Your MERCY. Amen.

Divine Mercy

The message and devotion of the Divine Mercy is based on the apparitions of Jesus to Sr. Maria Faustina of the Most Blessed Sacrament in Poland beginning in 1931.

According to the Diary of Saint Faustina, Jesus said, "Paint an image according to the pattern you see, with the inscription: Jesus, I trust in You.

I desire that this image be venerated, first in your chapel, then throughout the world".

In 1935, an inner voice taught her the prayer of Divine Mercy and Jesus told her, "Say unceasingly the chaplet that I have taught you".

He also asked her to pray at three o'clock each afternoon and to "Immerse yourself in My Passion". Devotion to the Divine Mercy spread even before the death of Sr. Faustina in 1938.

However, around 1959, the Church prohibited the spread of the devotion due to inaccurate information and confusing translations of the Diary.

Through the persistence of the Archbishop of Krakow, almost twenty years later, Cardinal Karol Wojtyla had the evidence re-evaluated and the Church reversed its earlier decision.

The message that Jesus gave to Sr. Faustina is one of complete love and mercy for poor sinners and for every soul that will draw near to Him. "My mercy is greater than your sins, and those of the entire world."

He says, "I let my Sacred Heart be pierced with a lance , thus opening wide the source of mercy for you. Come with trust to draw graces from this fountain." Jesus calls upon us to trust Him, to receive His mercy and to let it flow to others. "No soul that has called upon my Mercy has ever been disappointed".

❖ **Feast Day:** Second Sunday of Easter
❖ **Name Meaning:** Mercy of Christ

NOVENA TO THE DIVINE MERCY

First Day

*"Today bring to Me all mankind, especially all sinners,
and immerse them in the ocean of My mercy.
In this way you will console Me in the bitter grief into
which the loss of souls plunges Me".*

Most Merciful Jesus, whose very nature it is to have compassion on us and to forgive us, do not look upon our sins but upon our trust which we place in Your infinite goodness.

Receive us all into the abode of Your Most Compassionate Heart, and never let us escape from It.

We beg this of You by Your love which unites You to the Father and the Holy Spirit.

Eternal Father, turn Your merciful gaze upon all mankind and especially upon poor sinners, all enfolded in the Most Compassionate Heart of Jesus.

For the sake of His sorrowful Passion show us Your mercy, that we may praise the omnipotence of Your mercy for ever and ever. Amen.

Second Day

*"Today bring to Me the Souls of Priests and Religious
and immerse them in My unfathomable mercy.
It was they who gave me strength to endure
My bitter Passion. Through them as through
channels My mercy flows out upon mankind".*

Most Merciful Jesus, from whom comes all that is good, increase Your grace in men and women consecrated to Your service, that they may perform worthy works of mercy; and that all who see them may glorify the Father of Mercy who is in heaven.

Eternal Father, turn Your merciful gaze upon the company of chosen ones in Your vineyard – upon the souls of priests and religious; and endow them with the strength of Your blessing.

For the love of the Heart of Your Son in which they are enfolded, impart to them Your power and light, that they may be able to guide others in the way of salvation and with one voice sing praise to Your boundless mercy for ages without end. Amen.

Third Day

"Today bring to Me all Devout and Faithful Souls,
and immerse them in the ocean of My mercy.
Those souls brought me consolation on
the Way of the cross. They were a drop of
consolation in the midst of an ocean of bitterness".

Most Merciful Jesus, from the treasury of Your mercy You impart your graces in great abundance to each and all. Receive into the abode of Your Most Compassionate Heart and never let us escape from it.

We beg this grace of You by that most wondrous love for the heavenly Father with which Your Heart burns so fiercely.

Eternal Father, turn your merciful gaze upon faithful souls, as upon the inheritance of Your Son. For the sake of His sorrowful Passion, grant them Your blessing and surround them with Your constant protection.

Thus may they never fail in love or lose the treasure of the holy faith, but rather, with all the hosts of Angels and Saints, may they glorify your boundless mercy for endless ages. Amen.

Fourth Day

*Today bring to Me those who do not believe in God
and those who do not know Me,
I was thinking also of them during My bitter Passion, and
their future zeal comforted My heart.
Immerse them in the ocean of My mercy".*

Most compassionate Jesus, You are the Light of the whole world. Receive into the abode of Your Most Compassionate Heart the souls of those who do not believe in God and of those who as yet do not know You.

Let the rays of Your grace enlighten them that they, too, together with us, may extol Your wonderful mercy, and do not let them escape from the abode which is Your Most Compassionate Heart.

Eternal Father, turn Your merciful gaze upon the souls of those who do not believe in You, and of those who as yet do not know You, but who are enclosed in the Most Compassionate Heart of Jesus.

Draw them to the light of the Gospel. These souls do not know what great happiness it is to love You. Grant that they, too, may extol the generosity of Your mercy for endless ages. Amen.

Fifth Day

*Today bring to Me the Souls of those who have
separated themselves from My Church*,
and immerse them in the ocean of My mercy.
During My bitter Passion they tore at My Body
and Heart, that is, My Church.
As they return to unity with the Church My wounds heal
and in this way they alleviate My Passion."*

Most Merciful Jesus, Goodness Itself, You do not refuse light to those who seek it of You.

Receive into the abode of Your Most Compassionate Heart the souls of those who have separated themselves from Your Church. Draw them by Your light into the unity of the Church, and do not let them escape from the abode of Your Most Compassionate Heart; but bring it about that they, too, come to glorify the generosity of Your mercy.

Eternal Father, turn Your merciful gaze upon the souls of those who have separated themselves from Your Son's Church, who have squandered Your blessings and misused Your graces by obstinately persisting in their errors.

Do not look upon their errors, but upon the love of Your own Son and upon His bitter Passion, which He underwent for their sake, since they, too, are enclosed in His Most Compassionate Heart. Bring it about that they also may glorify Your great mercy for endless ages. Amen.

Sixth Day

Today bring to Me the Meek and Humble Souls
and the Souls of Little Children,
and immerse them in My mercy. These souls most closely
resemble My Heart. They strengthened Me during
My bitter agony. I saw them as earthly Angels, who will
keep vigil at My altars. I pour out upon them whole torrents
of grace. I favor humble souls with My confidence.

Most Merciful Jesus, You yourself have said, "Learn from Me for I am meek and humble of heart." Receive into the abode of Your Most Compassionate Heart all meek and humble souls and the souls of little children. These souls send all heaven into ecstasy and they are the heavenly Father's favorites. They are a sweet-smelling bouquet before the throne of God; God himself takes delight in their fragrance. These souls have a permanent abode in Your Most Compassionate Heart, O Jesus, and they unceasingly sing out a hymn of love and mercy.

Eternal Father, turn Your merciful gaze upon meek souls, upon humble souls, and upon little children who are enfolded in the abode which is the Most Compassionate Heart of Jesus. These souls bear the closest resemblance to Your Son. Their fragrance rises from the earth and reaches Your very throne. Father of mercy and of all goodness, I beg You by the love You bear these souls and by the delight You take in them: Bless the whole world, that all souls together may sing out the praises of Your mercy for endless ages. Amen.

Seventh Day

Today bring to Me the Souls who especially venerate and glorify My Mercy*, and immerse them in My mercy. These souls sorrowed most over my Passion and entered most deeply into My spirit. They are living images of My Compassionate Heart. These souls will shine with a special brightness in the next life. Not one of them will go into the fire of Hell. I shall particularly defend each one of them at the hour of death.

Most Merciful Jesus, whose Heart is Love Itself, receive into the abode of Your Most Compassionate Heart the souls of those who particularly extol and venerate the greatness of Your mercy. These souls are mighty with the very power of God Himself. In the midst of all afflictions and adversities they go forward, confident of Your mercy; and united to You, O Jesus, they carry all mankind on their shoulders. These souls will not be judged severely, but Your mercy will embrace them as they depart from this life. Eternal Father, turn Your merciful gaze upon the souls who glorify and venerate Your greatest attribute, that of Your fathomless mercy, and who are enclosed in the Most Compassionate Heart of Jesus. These souls are a living Gospel; their hands are full of deeds of mercy, and their hearts, overflowing with joy, sing a canticle of mercy to You, O Most High! I beg You O God: Show them Your mercy according to the hope and trust they have placed in You. Let there be accomplished in them the promise of Jesus, who said to them that during their life, but especially at the hour of death, the souls who will venerate this fathomless mercy of His, He, Himself, will defend as His glory. Amen.

Eighth Day

Today bring to Me the Souls who are in the prison of Purgatory, and immerse them in the abyss of My mercy. Let the torrents of My Blood cool down their scorching flames. All these souls are greatly loved by Me. They are making retribution to My justice. It is in your power to bring them relief. Draw all the indulgences from the treasury of My Church and offer them on their behalf. Oh, if you only knew the torments they suffer, you would continually offer for them the alms of the spirit and pay off their debt to My justice."

Most merciful Jesus, You Yourself have said that You desire mercy; so I bring into the abode of Your Most Compassionate Heart the souls in Purgatory, souls who are very dear to You, and yet, who must make retribution to Your justice. May the streams of Blood and Water which gushed forth from Your Heart put out the flames of Purgatory, that there, too, the power of Your mercy may be celebrated.

Eternal Father, turn Your merciful gaze upon the souls suffering in Purgatory, who are enfolded in the Most Compassionate Heart of Jesus.

I beg You, by the sorrowful Passion of Jesus Your Son, and by all the bitterness with which His most sacred Soul was flooded: Manifest Your mercy to the souls who are under Your just scrutiny. Look upon them in no other way but only through the Wounds of Jesus, Your dearly beloved Son; for we firmly believe that there is no limit to Your goodness and compassion. Amen.

Ninth Day

*Today bring to Me the Souls who have become Lukewarm,
and immerse them in the abyss of My mercy.
These souls wound My Heart most painfully. My soul suffered
the most dreadful loathing in the Garden of Olives because
of lukewarm souls. They were the reason I cried out:
"Father, take this cup away from Me, if it be Your will."
For them, the last hope of salvation is to run to My mercy."*

Most Compassionate Jesus, You are Compassion Itself. I bring lukewarm souls into the abode of Your Most Compassionate Heart. In this fire of Your pure love let these tepid souls, who, like corpses, filled You with such deep loathing, be once again set aflame.

O Most Compassionate Jesus, exercise the omnipotence of Your mercy and draw them into the very ardor of Your love, and bestow upon them the gift of holy love, for nothing is beyond Your power.

Eternal Father, turn Your merciful gaze upon lukewarm souls who are nonetheless enfolded in the Most Compassionate Heart of Jesus. Father of Mercy, I beg You by the bitter Passion of Your Son and by His three hour agony on the Cross: Let them, too, glorify the abyss of Your mercy. Amen.

THE CHAPLET OF THE DIVINE MERCY

Opening Prayer: *You expired, O Jesus, but the source of life gushed forth for souls and an ocean of mercy opened up for the world. O Fount of Life, unfathomable Divine Mercy, envelop the whole world and empty Yourself out upon us. O Blood and Water, which gushed forth from the Heart of Jesus as a fount of mercy for us, I trust in You. Amen*

(For recitation on ordinary rosary beads)

Our Father..., Hail Mary..., The Apostles' Creed.
Then, on the OUR FATHER BEADS YOU WILL SAY THE FOLLOWING WORDS:
Eternal Father, I offer You the Body and Blood, Soul and Divinity of Your dearly beloved Son, Our Lord Jesus Christ, in atonement for our sins and those of the whole world.
On the HAIL MARY BEADS
you will say the following words:
For the sake of His sorrowful Passion have mercy on us and on the whole world.
In conclusion THREE TIMES *you will recite these words:*
Holy God, Holy Mighty One, Holy Immortal One, have mercy on us and on the whole world.

Closing Prayer: *Eternal God in whom Mercy is endless and the treasury of Compassion inexhaustible, look kindly upon us and increase your Mercy in us so that in difficult moments we might not despair not become despondent, but with great confidence, submit ourselves to Your Holy Will, which is Love and Mercy itself.*

3 O'CLOCK PRAYER

At Three O'clock, implore My mercy, especially for sinners; and, if only for a brief moment, immerse yourself in My Passion, particularly in My abandonment at the moment of agony. This is the hour of great mercy... In this hour I will refuse nothing to the soul that makes a request of Me in virtue of My Passion.

As often as you hear the clock strike the third hour immerse yourself completely in My mercy, adoring and glorifying it, invoke it's omnipotence for the whole world, and particularly for poor sinners, for at that moment mercy was opened wide for every soul. In this hour you can obtain everything for yourself and for others for the asking; it was the hour of grace for the whole world–mercy triumphed over justice.

Try your best make the Stations of the Cross in this hour, provided that your duties permit it; and if you are not able to make the Stations of the Cross, then at least step into the chapel for a moment and adore, in the Most Blessed Sacrament. My Heart, which is full of mercy: and should you be unable to step into a chapel, immerse yourself in prayer wherever you happen to be, if only for a very brief instant.

LITANY TO THE DIVINE MERCY

Lord, have mercy.	Christ, have mercy.
Lord, have mercy on us,	Christ, have mercy.
Christ, hear us,	Christ, graciously hear us.
God the Father of Heaven,	have mercy on us.
God the Son,	
Redeemer of the world,	have mercy on us.
God the Holy Spirit,	have mercy on us.
Holy Trinity, one God,	have mercy on us.
Heart of Jesus,	
Son of the Eternal Father,	"
Heart of Jesus,	
formed by the Holy Spirit in the womb of the Virgin Mother,	"
Heart of Jesus,	
one with the eternal Word,	"
Heart of Jesus,	
infinite in majesty,	"
Heart of Jesus,	
holy temple of God,	"
Heart of Jesus,	
tabernacle of the Most High,	"
Heart of Jesus,	
house of God and gate of heaven,	"
Heart of Jesus,	
aflame with love for us,	"
Heart of Jesus,	
source of justice and love,	"
Heart of Jesus,	
full of goodness and love,	"

Heart of Jesus,
  wellspring of all virtue,   have mercy on us.
Heart of Jesus,
  worthy of all praise   "
Heart of Jesus,
  king and center of all hearts,   "
Heart of Jesus,
  treasure house of wisdom
  and knowledge,   "
Heart of Jesus,
  in whom there dwells
  the fullness of God,   "
Heart of Jesus,
  in whom the Father is well pleased, "
Heart of Jesus,
  from whose fullness
  we have all received,   "
Heart of Jesus,
  desire of the eternal hills,   "
Heart of Jesus,
  patient and full of mercy,   "
Heart of Jesus,
  generous to all who turn to You,   "
Heart of Jesus,
  fountain of life and holiness,   "
Heart of Jesus,
  atonement for our sins,   "
Heart of Jesus,
  overwhelmed with insults,   "
Heart of Jesus,
  broken for our sins,   "

OUR LADY OF DIVINE MERCY

Heart of Jesus,
    obedient even to death,   have mercy on us.
Heart of Jesus,
    pierced by a lance,   "
Heart of Jesus,
    source of all consolation,   "
Heart of Jesus,
    our life and resurrection,   "
Heart of Jesus,
    victim for our sins   "
Heart of Jesus,
    hope of all who die in You,   "
Heart of Jesus,
    delight of all the saints,
    victim for our sins   "

Lamb of God, Who takes away the sins of the world,
    Spare us, O Lord.
Lamb of God, Who takes away the sins of the world,
    Graciously hear us, O Lord,
Lamb of God, Who takes away the sins of the world,
    Have mercy on us.

    V. Jesus, gentle and humble of heart.
    R. Touch our hearts and make them like Your own.

LET US PRAY

Defend, we request You, O Lord, through the intercession
of the Blessed Mary ever Virgin, this family from all
adversity; and, as in all humility they prostrate hemselves
before You, do You mercifully protect them against all the
snares of their enemies; through Christ our Lord. Amen.

Jesus Christ the King

Prayer to
Jesus Christ the King

Almighty everlasting God,
who in Thy beloved Son,
King of the whole world,
hast willed to restore
all things a new;
grant in Thy mercy
that all the families of nations,
rent asunder by
the wound of sin,
may be subjected to
His most gentle rule.
Who with Thee liveth
and reigneth
world without end.
Amen.
(Roman Missal)

Jesus Christ the King

Christ the King is one of the names of Jesus found in various forms in Scripture. He is referred to as King Eternal, King of Israel, King of the Jews, King of kings and King of the Ages.

The Feast of Christ the King was instituted by Pope Pius XI in his encyclical Quas Primas in 1925. As a response to the rise of secularism and unrest between nations, Pope Pius stated, "Men must look for the peace of Christ in the Kingdom of Christ."

He sited throughout the Scriptures that Christ is the King, come out of Jacob to rule, sent by the Father as king over Zion, future King of Israel and ruler from sea to sea. The Prophets spoke of His reign and His kingdom and His power and His mercy.

In the New Testament, the angel said to Mary, "Great will be His dignity and He will be called Son of the Most High. The Lord God will give Him the throne of David His father.

He will rule over the house of Jacob forever and His reign will be without end."

Pope Pius further stated, "It was surely right, then, in view of the common teachings of the sacred books, that the Catholic Church, which is the kingdom of Christ on earth, destined to be spread among all men and all nations, should with every token of veneration salute her Author and Founder in her liturgy as King and Lord, and as King of Kings."

When humanity recognizes Christ as King, the world will receive the "great blessings of real liberty, well-ordered discipline, peace and harmony". The Feast was set on the last Sunday in October but was changed during the calendar reforms after the Second Vatican Council.

Prince of Peace

Jesus is the Prince of Peace. In the Old Testament, the prophet Isaiah describes to us He who is to come as the child, the Son given to us, named "Wonder-Counselor, God-Hero, Father-Forever, Prince of Peace." The world, a vast territory, rests on His shoulders.

To have peace is to have harmony between people and to experience a sense of security.

Jesus comes to teach us how to live with one another in harmony.

He gives us His laws, His Commandments, so that we can love one another and live in peace and tranquility.

All through the New Testament Jesus teaches us, by example, ways to live in peace with our families and our neighbors and even our enemies. He instructs us to love one another, to pray for one another, to turn the other cheek, to give to those who ask, to clothe, to feed, to care for and to visit. He brings peace in the storm and cures those who are possessed and heals the sick.

On His last night with His disciples, Jesus tells them, "Peace I leave with you; my peace I give to you. Not as the world gives do I give it to you."

Jesus is the Son of the One who rules over all; who has supreme authority.

His life is the model for us to live in peace. He reconciles us to God and with one another.

As Prince of Peace, Jesus calls us to work for justice and to work in charity and love.

Christ the Teacher

Prayer to Christ the Teacher

O source of all Wisdom,
Christ the Teacher
You are the Way,
the Truth, and the Life.
Teach me to embrace the truths
You have revealed to Your Church.
Fill my soul with Your Grace
that I may love God above all
and my neighbor as myself.
Christ Jesus, all Knowing
source of wisdom
bless me and teach me.
O Light of the world,
teach me always to follow You
that I should not walk in darkness,
but have forever
the Light of Knowledge.
Amen.

Christ the Teacher

From His youth to His death and Resurrection, Christ is our teacher. We read about the boy Jesus at age twelve in the Gospel of Luke, "After three days they found him in the temple, sitting in the midst of the teachers, listening to them and asking them questions, and all who heard him were astounded at his understanding and his answers."

Christ as teacher is often depicted with His hand raised in blessing and His opposite hand holding a Book of the Gospels, filled with His teachings. His actions and His words teach us. From the beginning of His ministry He taught in the synagogues around Galilee.

He teaches the Beatitudes in the Sermon on the Mount to the crowds of people who gather. He teaches us the Laws about adultery, divorce, anger and retaliation, "When someone strikes you on your right cheek, turn the other one to him as well."

He talks to us about tithing and fasting and treasure, "For where your treasure is, there also will be your heart."

He teaches love and prayer and the golden rule. By His example, He cures, calms, heals and cleanses. He fasts and He prays and He loves and He commissions. He teaches us by His Parables so that we can more fully understand Him.

"This is why I speak to them in parables, because 'they look but do not see and hear but do not listen or understand.'" In the Gospel of John He refers to Himself as teacher. "You call me teacher and that is rightfully so." He teaches us what it truly means to love and to give of oneself for another.

In His final lesson as teacher, He lays down His life for us and dies on the cross and as He has promised, He returns and leaves us with the gift of His Spirit.

The Good Shepherd

Prayer to
The Good Shepherd

Almighty and ever-living God,
by the blood of the eternal covenant
you brought again from
the dead our Lord Jesus,
that great shepherd of the sheep;
make us perfect in every good work,
and work in us that which
is pleasing and good;
give us new strength from
the courage of Christ our shepherd,
and lead us to join the saints in heaven.
through Jesus Christ to whom be glory
for ever and ever who is alive with
with You and the Holy Spirit,
one God now and for ever.
Amen

The Good Shepherd

Jesus refers to Himself as the Good Shepherd in many places in Holy Scripture. A shepherd is one who feeds and guards his sheep, especially those in large flocks.

Sheep tend to put themselves in danger by wandering from the flock. Jesus, as the Good Shepherd, in John 10, "lays down his life for the sheep." He dies on the cross so we can be saved.

He knows His sheep and calls them each by name. Those who work strictly because they get paid will not stay with the task in times of trouble or hardship.

In the Gospels of Matthew and Luke we read that Jesus wants to save every single one of us. He is the Good Shepherd who is always ready to lead us back no matter the danger or how far we wander from Him. In the Gospel of John we read that He wants to leave no one behind whether they are a part of His fold or not.

He came to save us all. Jesus also tells Peter "Feed my sheep." He passes on to Peter the responsibility of caring for His flock.

The Latin word for shepherd is "Pastor" which is the term used for many of the clergy. They are called to "shepherd" their flock, the people of their community.

Jesus laid down His life and rose again to open the gates for us, His flock. As our Shepherd, He does not abandon us.

He feeds us and He guards us and He seeks any who wander away from Him. Jesus is the Good Shepherd. Good Shepherd Sunday is the fourth Sunday of Easter.

Prayer to Christ, the High Priest

O God, who,

while the disciples

were worshiping and fasting,

ordered Saul and Barnabas

to be set apart for the work

to which You had called them,

be present now

to Your Church in prayer, and You,

who know the hearts of all,

indicate those whom You have

chosen for ministry.

Through Christ our Lord.

Amen.

Christ, the High Priest

igh Priest is one of the many titles given to Jesus Christ. "Therefore since we have a great High Priest who has passed through the Heavens, Jesus, the Son of God, let us hold fast to our confession."

Heb.4, 14 The Book of Hebrews in the New Testament explains this title of Jesus as High Priest. Jesus is faithful to the One, His Father, who has appointed Him. Just as Moses was a faithful servant so Jesus is the faithful Son placed over the people of God. He understands our temptations because He too was tempted yet remained sinless. "For we do not have a High Priest who is unable to sympathize with our weaknesses, but one who has similarly been tested in every way, yet without sin." Heb.4, 15 Jesus is declared by God to be our High Priest according to the order of Melchizedek. Though the high priests of the Old Covenant prefigure the Priesthood of Jesus, they cannot continue as our priests because they die, but Jesus remains forever. He is always here to save us and always here to intercede for us to the Father if we come to Him.

In the Old Testament, the high priest was taken from among men and they offered sacrifices at the altar to atone for the sins of themselves and the people. Jesus has no need to offer sacrifices day after day as they did.

He offered Himself once and for all on the day He died for us.

He was made perfect and He is our mediator for a New Covenant. His own blood obtained eternal redemption. When we confess our sins, we reconcile ourselves to God the Father through Jesus His Son, as our High Priest.

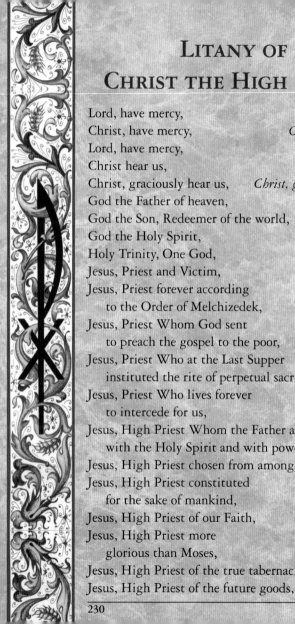

LITANY OF
CHRIST THE HIGH PRIEST

Lord, have mercy,	*Lord, have mercy*
Christ, have mercy,	*Christ, have mercy*
Lord, have mercy,	*Lord, have mercy*
Christ hear us,	*Christ hear us*
Christ, graciously hear us,	*Christ, graciously hear us*
God the Father of heaven,	*Have mercy on us*
God the Son, Redeemer of the world,	"
God the Holy Spirit,	"
Holy Trinity, One God,	"
Jesus, Priest and Victim,	*Have mercy on us*
Jesus, Priest forever according to the Order of Melchizedek,	"
Jesus, Priest Whom God sent to preach the gospel to the poor,	"
Jesus, Priest Who at the Last Supper instituted the rite of perpetual sacrifice,	"
Jesus, Priest Who lives forever to intercede for us,	"
Jesus, High Priest Whom the Father anointed with the Holy Spirit and with power,	"
Jesus, High Priest chosen from among men,	"
Jesus, High Priest constituted for the sake of mankind,	"
Jesus, High Priest of our Faith,	"
Jesus, High Priest more glorious than Moses,	"
Jesus, High Priest of the true tabernacle,	"
Jesus, High Priest of the future goods,	"

Jesus, High Priest, Who are holy,
innocent, and undefiled,   *Have mercy on us*
Jesus, High Priest faithful and merciful,   ”
Jesus, High Priest inflamed
with zeal for God and souls,   ”
Jesus, High Priest made perfect forever,   ”
Jesus, High Priest, Who by Your own
Blood entered into the heavens,   ”
Jesus, High Priest,
Who have opened for us a new way,   ”
Jesus, High Priest, Who have loved us
and washed us from our sins in Your Blood,   ”
Jesus, High Priest, Who offered Yourself
to God as an oblation and victim,   ”
Jesus, Sacrifice of God and men,   ”
Jesus, holy and immaculate offering,   ”
Jesus, pleasing victim,   ”
Jesus, peace offering,   ”
Jesus, sacrifice of propitiation and praise,   ”
Jesus, offering of reconciliation and peace,   ”
Jesus, offering in which we place
our trust and have access to God,   ”
From presumptions entrance
into the clergy,   *Deliver us, O Jesus*
From the sin of sacrilege,   ”
From the spirit of incontinence,   ”
From base pursuits,   ”
From all stain of simony,   ”
From the unworthy distribution
of the goods of the Church,   ”
From the love of the world and its vanities,   ”
From the unworthy celebration of Your Mysteries,   ”

231

By Your eternal priesthood, *Deliver us, O Jesus*

By the holy anointing whereby You were
    constituted a priest by God the Father,   "

By Your priestly spirit,   "

By that ministry whereby You
    glorified Your Father on earth,   "

By Your bloody immolation
    realized once and for all upon the Cross,   "

By that same sacrifice renewed daily upon the altar,   "

By that divine power which
    You invisibly exercise in Your priests,   "

Deign to conserve the whole priestly
    order in holy religion, *We beseech You, hear us*

Deign to provide Your people
    with pastors after Your own heart,   "

Deign to fill them with
    the spirit of Your priesthood,   "

Grant that the lips of the priests
    might preserve true knowledge,   "

Deign to send faithful workers into Your harvest,   "

Deign to multiply the faithful ministers of
Your Mysteries,   "

Grant that they religiously
    persevere in the service of Your will,   "

Grant them meekness in the ministry,
shrewdness in action, and constancy in prayer,   "

Grant that the cult of the Most Blessed
    Sacrament be promoted everywhere by them,   "

Deign to receive those
    who served You well into Your joy,   "

Lamb of God, Who take away the sin of the world,
spare us, O Lord

Lamb of God, Who take away the sin of the world,
graciously hear us, O Lord

Lamb of God, Who take away the sin of the world,
have mercy on us, O Lord

Jesus, Priest, *hear us*
Jesus, Priest, *graciously hear us*

LET US PRAY

*God, Sanctifier
and Protector of Your Church,
raise up in her through
Your Spirit fitting
and faithful administrators
of the Holy Mysteries,
so that through their ministry
and example the Christian people may
be led under Your protection
along the way of salvation.
Through Christ our Lord.
Amen.*

An Act of Reparation for Blasphemies Against the Holy Name

O Jesus, Son of the living God, our Savior and Redeemer, behold us prostrate at Your feet.

We beg pardon, and make this act of reparation for all the blasphemies uttered against Your Holy Name, for all the outrages committed against You in the most Holy Sacrament of the altar, for all irreverence shown to Your most blessed and immaculate Mother, and for all the calumnies spoken against Your Spouse, our holy mother, the Catholic Church. O Jesus, who said: "Whatever you shall ask the Father in My Name, that He will do," we pray and beseech You for our brethren who are living in danger of sin, that You would preserve them from the seductions of apostasy.

Save them who stand over the abyss; give them light and knowledge of the truth, power and strength in the conflict against evil, and perseverance in faith and active charity.

And therefore, most merciful Jesus, do we pray to the Father in Your Name, with Whom You live and reign in unity with the Holy Spirit forever and ever.

Amen

LITANY OF THE
MOST HOLY NAME OF JESUS

Lord,	*have mercy.*
Christ,	"
Lord,	"
Jesus,	*hear us.*
Jesus,	*graciously hear us.*
God, the Father of Heaven,	*have mercy on us.*
God, the Son, Redeemer of the world,	"
God, the Holy Spirit, Holy Trinity, one God,	
Jesus, Son of the living God,	
Jesus, Splendor of the Father,	"
Jesus, Brightness of eternal light,	"
Jesus, King of glory,	"
Jesus, Sun of justice,	"
Jesus, Son of the Virgin Mary,	"
Jesus, most amiable,	"
Jesus, most admirable,	"
Jesus, mighty God,	"
Jesus, Father of the world to come,	"
Jesus, Angel of great counsel,	"
Jesus, most powerful,	"
Jesus, most patient,	"
Jesus, most obedient,	"
Jesus, meek and humble of heart,	"
Jesus, Lover of chastity,	"
Jesus, Lover of us,	"
Jesus, God of peace,	"
Jesus, Author of life,	"
Jesus, Example of virtues,	"
Jesus, zealous Lover of souls,	"
Jesus, our God,	"
Jesus, our Refuge,	"

Jesus, Father of the poor, *have mercy on us.*
Jesus, Treasure of the faithful, "
Jesus, Good Shepherd, "
Jesus, True Light, "
Jesus, Eternal Wisdom, "
Jesus, infinite Goodness, "
Jesus, our Way and our Life, "
Jesus, Joy of Angels, "
Jesus, King of Patriarchs, "
Jesus, Master of the Apostles, "
Jesus, Teacher of the Evangelists, "
Jesus, Strength of Martyrs, "
Jesus, Light of Confessors, "
Jesus, Purity of Virgins, "
Jesus, Crown of all Saints, "
Be merciful to us: *Spare us, O Jesus.*
Be merciful to us: *Graciously hear us, O Jesus.*
From all evil, *O Jesus, deliver us.*
From all sin, "
From Your wrath, "
From the snares of the devil, "
From the spirit of fornication, "
From everlasting death, "
From the neglect of Your inspirations, "
Through the mystery of
    Your Holy Incarnation, "
Through Your Nativity, "
Through Your Infancy, "
Through Your most Divine Life, "
Through Your labors, "
Through Your Agony and Passion, "
Through Your Cross and Dereliction, "
Through Your Pains and Torments, "
Through Your Death and Burial, "
Through Your Resurrection, "

238

Through Your Ascension,   *O Jesus, deliver us.*
Through Your Institution of the
    most Holy Eucharist,   ,,
Through Your Joy,   ,,
Through Your Glory,   ,,

Lamb of God, You take away the sins of the world:
                                            Spare us, O Jesus.
Lamb of God, You take away the sins of the world:
                                    Graciously hear us, O Jesus.
Lamb of God, You take away the sins of the world:
                                    Have mercy on us, O Jesus.
Jesus, hear us.
Jesus, graciously hear us.

LET US PRAY

Lord Jesus Christ, You;
have said: "Ask, and you shall receive;
seek, and you shall find; knock,
and it shall be opened to you":
give, we beg You, to us who ask,
the grace of Your most Divine Love,
that with all our hearts, words,
and works, we may love You,
and never cease to praise You.
Lord, grant us an abiding reverence
and love of Your Holy Name,
for You never abandon those who are Yours.
You, who lives and reigns forever.
Amen.